ALBERTA'S CENTENNIAL

A Celebration!

Acknowledgements

The publishers of *Alberta's Centennial – a Celebration!* wish to
acknowledge the significant contributions of the many people
and organizations that provided material for this book.
The publishers also wish to thank all those who assisted
and contributed to the book.

TABLE OF CONTENTS

FOREWORD 11

REMEMBERING OUR PAST 12

SETTING THE STAGE 20

CAPTURING THE SPIRIT 32

A CELEBRATION FIT FOR A QUEEN 58

THE PARTY OF THE CENTURY 82

SPREADING THE JOY 150

SHARING THE LIMELIGHT 158

SOUVENIRS AND HONOURS 166

LASTING LEGACIES 176

ALBERTA'S CENTENNIAL BY THE NUMBERS . .194

Alberta's Centennial – a Celebration!

"This country fascinates me. There is wine in the air; a feeling of excitement, of expectancy... and the conviction grows that great things are bound to happen in this rich new country."

DR. HENRY MARSHALL TORY, FIRST PRESIDENT OF THE UNIVERSITY OF ALBERTA, 1906

FOREWORD

Albertans Did it Their Way

What a year! In 2005, Albertans had a once-in-a-lifetime opportunity to mark a
century of accomplishment as a people and as a province. It was a time to celebrate
our past, imagine our future, and Albertans did it with enthusiasm and pride.

While there were dozens of provincially led Centennial initiatives and celebrations,
it was the grassroots efforts of Albertans that truly made 2005 a year to remember.
In over 300 communities, from Fort Chipewyan to Milk River, thousands of
people caught the spirit and ran with it. From family reunions, homecomings
and fairs, to parades, plays, and picnics, Albertans made the Centennial their
own in countless meaningful ways.

The scope of our Centennial celebration demonstrates just how much creativity,
energy and pride there is in this province. As Albertans go on to achieve great
things, I am confident our next century will be as successful as our last.

This keepsake of our Centennial year cannot possibly do justice to all the people,
communities and organizations that contributed to Alberta's 100th birthday.
Rather, the photographs and events shown here are meant to capture just some
of the special moments of our Centennial celebrations, and most importantly,
our Alberta spirit.

Ralph Klein

Ralph Klein, Premier of Alberta

Remembering Our Past

What a century! In 1905 Alberta was a sparsely settled, rural agricultural province. One hundred years later it is Canada's energy powerhouse. The story of how we got here is filled with memorable dates, famous people and great achievements. But just as important are everyday efforts of the countless ordinary people who made Alberta what it is today.

Prime Minister Sir Wilfrid Laurier addresses the crowd at Alberta's inaugural ceremonies.

Alberta becomes a province

September 1, 1905, was a day to remember in Edmonton. Alberta officially became a province and the people were in a partying mood. There were parades, speeches, and a 21-gun salute, and the Royal North West Mounted Police performed their musical ride. The festivities began the night before with a grand concert at the Thistle Rink attended by Governor General Earl Grey. Prime Minister Sir Wilfrid Laurier spoke at the inaugural ceremonies on the big day. The crowds were entertained with a parade down Jasper Avenue, horse races, baseball games, lacrosse and polo. Later, more than a thousand invited guests danced the night away at the inaugural ball.

Tourists, Aboriginal peoples, railroad workers and city dwellers were all part of Alberta's cultural mix around the turn of the last century.

Who we are and where we came from

Starting with the Aboriginal first Albertans, people the world over have been attracted to this land and its opportunities. The earliest settlers were mainly Eastern Canadian, European and American. Today's immigrants to Alberta might well speak Mandarin, Tagalog, Punjabi, Spanish, Urdu or Arabic as their first language. Newcomers from other parts of Canada add their own voices to the mix. Each group has contributed unique gifts to building our great province.

ALBERTA 1905 — 2005
100 AMAZING YEARS

How we got from there to here

A lot can happen in a hundred years. Triumphs. Tragedies. Booms. Busts. Albertans have seen it all. Here are some of the highlights of Alberta's amazing first century.

1918 – The Spanish influenza pandemic hits Alberta. A total of 38,000 cases, including 4,000 deaths, were reported.

1912 – Alberta Legislature Building opens on the site of Fort Edmonton.

1919 – Edward Prince of Wales (later Edward VIII) makes the first Royal Visit to Alberta and is so taken with Alberta's ranching country that he buys the Bedingfield Ranch (later renamed the E. P. Ranch).

1908 – University of Alberta is founded.

1907 – Jasper Forest National Park is established.

1915 – Legendary Edmonton Grads women's basketball team is formed and goes on to win an unrivalled 502 out of 522 games before disbanding in 1940.

1921 – The Scientific and Industrial Research Council of Alberta (later renamed the Alberta Research Council) becomes the first provincial research organization in Canada.

1905 – Alberta is inaugurated as a province on September 1 with Prime Minister Sir Wilfrid Laurier presiding.

1911 – Great Canadian Dinosaur Rush (1911-1925) begins as world famous fossil hunters compete to discover dinosaur bones in the Red Deer River valley.

1912 – First Calgary Stampede attracts competitors from all over North America. Alberta Aboriginal cowboy Tom Three Persons is crowned the world's bucking horse champion.

1916 – Father Lacombe dies after a lifetime of service to Alberta's Aboriginal people.

1906 – Alberta's first legislature officially opens in Edmonton's Thistle Rink arena.

1914 – Explosion in Hillcrest Mine in the Crowsnest Pass kills 189. The event was Canada's worst mine disaster.

1900

1910

1920

16

1936 – Alberta farmer Charles Noble develops the Noble blade cultivator, considered one of the most important agricultural inventions of the 20th century.

1942 – Edmonton becomes the staging ground for building the Alaska Highway during World War II.

1950 – Alberta government launches the Rat Patrol on the Saskatchewan border. The province has been rat-free ever since.

1930 – Alberta gains ownership of its natural resources from the federal government.

1955 – Province begins construction on the Jubilee auditoria in Edmonton and Calgary to celebrate Alberta's 50th anniversary.

1929 – "Famous Five" Alberta women win the case to recognize women as "persons" under Canadian law.

1938 – Métis Population Betterment Act establishes 12 Métis settlements in Alberta.

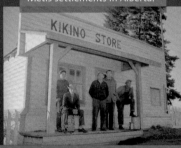

1929 – Karl Clark patents the hot water extraction method used to mine Alberta's oilsands today.

1929 – World War I flying ace Wilfrid "Wop" May and Vic Horner make an historic mercy flight in an open cockpit to deliver diphtheria serum from Edmonton to Fort Vermilion in the dead of winter.

1947 – Imperial Oil strikes oil with Leduc #1, beginning the modern oil industry in Canada and making Alberta a world-scale petroleum producer.

1930

1940

1950

1967 – Alberta's Provincial Museum and Archives opens in honour of Canada's centennial.

1979 – Alberta's population passes 2 million.

1958 – Alberta Blood Indian leader James Gladstone becomes Canada's first Aboriginal senator.

1980 – Alberta celebrates it 75th anniversary.

1968 – The Calgary Tower officially opens.

1977 – Calgary plays Metropolis in the movie Superman.

1963 – The Northern Alberta Institute of Technology (NAIT) officially opens.

1981 – Head-Smashed-In Buffalo Jump is designated a UNESCO World Heritage Site.

1974 – Ralph Steinhauer, former Chief of the Saddle Lake First Nation, is appointed Lieutenant Governor of Alberta, becoming the first Aboriginal Canadian to hold a vice-regal position.

1964 – The world's first commercial oilsands project, Great Canadian Oil Sands (now Suncor), begins construction, leading to explosive growth in Fort McMurray.

1981 – West Edmonton Mall opens as the world's largest shopping centre.

1957 – The first automobile trip from Edmonton to Fort McMurray takes 18 hours to complete.

1978 – Edmonton hosts the Commonwealth Games with Queen Elizabeth II performing the opening honours.

1960   1970   1980

1987 – Tornado leaves 27 people dead and over $300 million in damage in Edmonton.

1988 – Calgary hosts the Winter Olympic Games.

2001 – World Championships in Athletics are held in Edmonton.

2000 – University of Alberta's "Edmonton Protocol" makes news as the world's most successful islet cell transplant treatment for Type 1 diabetes.

1994 – Alberta figure skater Kurt Browning is inducted into the Canadian Sports Hall of Fame. Browning was the first skater in the world to land a quadruple jump in competition.

1984 – Edmonton Oilers score their first of five Stanley Cup wins over seven years.

2004 – Alberta announces the provincial debt will be eliminated in 2005.

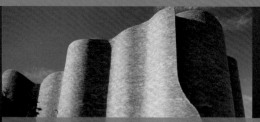

2005 – Alberta celebrates its Centennial.

1990 – Calgary-born architect Douglas Cardinal is awarded the Order of Canada. His undulating, natural style is easily recognized in many Alberta communities. The Canadian Museum of Civilization in Hull Quebec is considered to be his best work.

1998 – Author W.O. Mitchell, a longtime Alberta resident, dies in Calgary. Mitchell's works include Canadian classics such as *Who Has Seen the Wind* and *Jake and the Kid*.

1985 – Royal Tyrrell Museum opens near Drumheller. The museum is named for J.B. Tyrrell, who made the first major dinosaur fossil discovery in the area – an *Albertosaurus* skull found along the Red Deer River in 1884.

Setting the Stage

A party of centennial proportions doesn't happen overnight. Planning for Alberta's 100th birthday began nearly a decade earlier. A 100th Anniversary Strategy Committee chaired by Mrs. Colleen Klein and Mr. Jack Donahue asked Albertans how they wanted to mark the occasion. The response was loud and clear: the people of Alberta wanted more than a big party and spectacular fireworks. They wanted commemorative programs that focus on people, communities and partnerships – and legacies that will last long after the fireworks are over.

Grant programs were created to help municipalities, non-profit groups and the Province make memorable Centennial investments for future generations. Communities rolled up their sleeves and got to work planning and raising funds for their dream projects, ranging from new or renovated arenas, recreation facilities and cultural centres to libraries, parks and museums.

But Albertans didn't have to choose between levity and legacies. There would still be big parties and spectacular fireworks, too. The Alberta 2005 Centennial Initiative team set up a website and launched a host of events, programs and activities designed to inspire all Albertans to get involved. Meanwhile, communities, schools, organizations and individuals started planning festivities that would celebrate their own unique part in Alberta's first century.

Opposite: Lois Hole, Alberta's Lieutenant Governor and honourary Centennial Ambassador, takes part in the ceremony beginning the one-year countdown to Alberta's Centennial. Ms. Hole passed away on January 6, 2005.

The public celebrations got underway September 1, 2004, when hundreds of Albertans gathered at the Alberta Legislature to begin the one-year countdown to the province's Centennial. The stage was set for Alberta's big year.

Centennial Ambassadors spread the spirit

More than 100 Centennial Ambassadors from across Alberta volunteered to help spread the Centennial spirit. The Centennial Ambassadors represented a diverse range of ages and community interests. Their job was to inspire all Albertans, communities and groups to get involved.

They threw themselves into the task, visiting schools and seniors' lodges, meeting with community groups, helping organizations plan their own special Centennial tributes, and making sure Alberta's birthday would be front and centre in Albertans' minds.

Opposite: 1. Premier Ralph Klein tells of the celebrations to come. 2. Health and Wellness Minister Iris Evans (left) shares the anticipation at the beginning of the one-year countdown to Alberta's 100th birthday. 3. Asani, *a cappella* Aboriginal women's choir, entertains the crowd. 4. Wayne Cao, MLA, Calgary-Fort, is recognized for his work as chair of the Official Song Committee. 5. Premier Klein receives his own, customized Centennial football jersey from the Calgary Stampeders and the Edmonton Eskimos. 6. The late Lieutenant Governor Lois Hole speaks to the crowd with some of Alberta's Centennial Ambassadors in the foreground. **This Page:** Alberta's Centennial Ambassadors line up at the Legislature to begin the one-year countdown to Alberta's Centennial.

www.wow!

The Alberta Centennial website was the "go to" place where Albertans could post their Centennial events, find out what others were doing, catch up on the latest Centennial news, and listen to Alberta's official song. Photo galleries on the website provided a colourful replay of events as the year progressed.

Albertans also shared their memories, photographs and artifacts on the website. Their heartwarming tales and amusing anecdotes provided a window on the real people — the builders and survivors — behind Alberta's amazing century. They tell of incredible hardship, determination, simple pleasures, small

successes — and heartbreaking failures, too. The community of Olds rolls up its collective sleeve to raise a one-room schoolhouse in 1905; an immigrant loses his land during the Depression for lack of the final payment; a young boy thrills at the memory of his family's first trip to Alberta's dinosaur country; an immigrant from the Philippines gets her first taste of snow.

Taken together, Albertans' contributions to the website provide an eloquent informal history of our province. Three of the many stories submitted appear on the opposite page.

Edmonton's new swimming pool makes a splash
by Jocelyn Proby

On August 2, 1922, the hottest day in 20 years, Edmonton Mayor D. M. Duggan opened the South Side Pool, saying that nothing during his term of office gave him greater pleasure. A swimming pool had been needed for many years because of the many drownings in the North Saskatchewan River, he said.

Edmontonians celebrated the opening with swimming races and novelty events: apple and bucket races for boys; balloon races for girls; the ladies swam in nightcaps carrying candles and the men were expected to swim a pool length in their street clothes. The pool was on the south side of the North Saskatchewan River in what was Riverside Park, and is now Queen Elizabeth Park. The Edmonton Bulletin reported: "It is delightfully situated in what is generally recognized as the city's most beautiful park. The bath looked very inviting for the deep green of the water gave back reflections of the surrounding trees and conjured up images of sweet water nymphs disporting in forest recesses."

Dust in the wind
(As told by Alice Marquardt De Nio to her great-niece Randi Marquardt Berting. Alice was born in Medicine Hat on March 29, 1903, and died in Calgary on February 24, 1996. Alice married Ernie De Nio in 1929, the year the Depression began.)

"It was tough. There was hardly any work. Ernie worked at a mine....There was only work one day a week because no one wanted to buy the coal and the prices were very low. The whistle at the mine would blow once if there was work that day, three times if there wasn't any work. Sometimes they'd put up a big light if there was work."

"Eggs cost 10 cents a dozen. The government shipped dried cod from Nova Scotia on the train and gave it to the people. The land was so dry that the topsoil blew into four-foot high piles in the ditch. The air was thick with it. The dirt blew in through every crack in the houses, and was on the tables, in the food. It was awful. Lights were kept on all day because it was so black from the dust in the air. Food was scarce and expensive. We had to make homemade bean soup. There were soup-lines everywhere. People were so poor."

Stuck on the road to Grande Prairie
by G.A. Cooper

The Depression hit the farmers and merchants of the Peace River District hard. Early in 1937 my dad was sent to push sales for his company, and to try to collect on a few long overdue accounts. He had to cover the whole area so we drove up; 405 miles [in] a brand-new 1936 Ford coupe. In those days the road was paved to St. Albert. There was a bit of gravel from there to Westlock. The rest was just plain mud. Good old Alberta gumbo. When you got stuck in Alberta gumbo you were there until it dried out. Or until you could get someone with a team of horses to pull you out.

We made it to Slave Lake, where it goes right along the shore for miles and miles. The water was still rising, but you know my dad. We kept going, and that's where we got stuck. We were up to the axles in mud, the fenders were packed with mud, it was getting dark, the water was getting closer and closer, and we weren't going anywhere.

Anyway, we did stay there all night, and next morning someone did come along with a team of horses. Probably he knew there would be cars stuck in that spot. People were giving him two bits a car or something like that. A nice bit of change for a farmer in those days. And we finally got to Grande Prairie.

We're having a party and you're invited!

Albertans invited friends and family around the world
to come home for the Centennial celebrations through
personalized letters from the Premier. They submitted
the names and addresses of their prospective guests on
postcards depicting scenes of fun and fellowship from
Alberta's past. The Premier sent more than 30,000
invitations to people in 110 countries around the globe.

1, 2 & 3: Centennial Invitation
Program images depict treasured
moments from Alberta's past.

Bring the home team, home.

You couldn't feel your toes. But it didn't matter. The ice was clean and new, the bright Alberta sun was shining and you were on "the pond" with your pals. The crisp sound of metal carving ice, the slap of sticks ... cheers and laughter warmed your hearts, and frost appeared on eyelashes and the brim of your cap.

It was perfect.

Then and now

The Centennial Invitation Program image above, entitled Smoky Lake Street Hockey, was taken in 1939. The boys are, from left to right, John Gavinchuk, Billy Antoniuk, Warren Wilson, Fred O'Shann, Alex Lenko, and Mike Kinasewich. The photo is a celebration of friendship, community and, of course, hockey. At left, Gavinchuk and O'Shann pass the puck to Premier Ralph Klein in 2005.

Centennial Invitation contest winners

Ray and Jean Schmitt, right, of Calgary, participated in the Premier's Centennial Invitation Program and won a free trip for four friends to come and help them celebrate Alberta's Centennial. In a contest presented by TELUS, Albertans submitting the names of family and friends by June 29 were eligible for the draw. The winners received airfare and five nights' accommodation for four guests. The Schmitts invited friends from Salt Lake City, Utah, and Savoury Island, British Columbia, to join them in attending the University of Alberta's Homecoming to celebrate the 50th anniversary of their graduation.

Alberta is calling me

Every great occasion deserves a soundtrack. More than 300 Albertans took up the challenge to create an official song for the province's 100th birthday. Singer/songwriter Mary Kieftenbeld came up with the winning submission. Her song, *Alberta,* captured the unfettered optimism that has always characterized the people of this province. The Alberta Centennial website carried pop and country versions of *Alberta,* arranged and produced by Calgary-based producer Dave Pierce, for downloading along with sheet music for school and community singalongs. Every school, library and music association in the province received copies of the song on CD. Alberta is only the second province, after Newfoundland and Labrador, to have an official song.

ALBERTA

Flatlands, rollin' plains
Clear blue skies, prairie rains;
A tapestry of colours in the fall.
Snow covered mountain tops,
Wheat fields, canola crops;
Alberta has it all.

Alberta is calling me.
Home sweet home,
it's where I'm proud to be.
Alberta is calling me.
Livin' right I'm feelin' free.

First Nations built the land
Fur trade, way back then.
We've come a long way since that.
Agriculture, lumberjacks,
Oil derricks, natural gas;
There is no turnin' back.

Alberta is calling me.
Home sweet home,
it's where I'm proud to be.
Alberta is calling me.
Livin' right I'm feelin' free.

Culture diverse as it can be.
This is the land of opportunity.
Welcoming friends, night and day.
That's the way I pray Alberta stays.

Opposite and this page:
1 & 3. Singer/songwriter Mary Kieftenbeld, creator of Alberta's official song, sang the country version of *Alberta* on CD. 2. L to r: Wayne Cao, MLA, Calgary-Fort, chair of the Official Song Committee; Michael Carey, singer of the pop version of *Alberta*; and Dave Pierce, song arranger/producer.

3

Capturing the Spirit

There were no half measures when it came to celebrating Alberta's 100th birthday. The province's Centennial year was a high-spirited affair from beginning to end. Individuals, families, organizations, and whole communities came up with creative ways to mark the big year and made it their own.

More than 1,900 community-inspired events involving thousands of participants and hundreds of volunteers were posted on the Centennial's website calendar. Countless other Centennial activities took place in cities, towns, hamlets and schools across the province.

Communities get inspired

Albertans young and old captured the spirit. They held concerts, family reunions, tournaments, and fairs. They re-enacted history, raised funds for charity, and shared their culture. And they ate lots of birthday cake.

The multitude of annual festivals and events around the province also saluted Alberta's Centennial. The Calgary Stampede mounted a special grandstand show

Alberta: A Centennial Story. Edmonton's Klondike Days saluted the Centennial with an Alberta trade show and the Alberta Centennial Tattoo. Alberta's 100th birthday took centre stage at the 2005 Banff Summer Arts Festival, which featured the home-grown opera *Filumena*. The Canadian Finals Rodeo, held in Edmonton, celebrated the Centennial with a video looking back on the province's 100-year history.

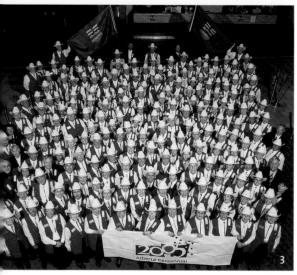

Opposite: 1. The Eastern Irrigation District celebrated its 70th anniversary in conjunction with Alberta's Centennial and won a red ribbon for its float in the Brooks and Bassano parade. 2. Centennial celebrants in Coleman dig into birthday cake. 3. The Medicine Hat Rodeo kicked things up a notch with a Centennial theme. 4. The community of Fort Macleod shows its festive colours. 5. Aboriginal performers provide entertainment at *A Touch of the Past* celebration at the Old Timers Cabin in Edmonton.

This page: 1. The community of Granum's Alberta Centennial cake was a work of art. 2. The Walker family of Trochu celebrated the 100th anniversary of the arrival of their ancestors George and Kate Walker to homestead in the area. 3. White Hat volunteers at Calgary International Airport went all out celebrating a century of their city's warm western hospitality. 4. Former Alberta Premier Peter Lougheed (r.) and his brother, Don, open a time capsule placed by their grandmother in the cornerstone of Central United (Methodist) Church in Calgary in 1904.

This page: 1. Arbour Lake 245 Beaver Colony held a special Centennial Celebration Night. 2. The Alberta Centennial Tattoo, held at Rexall Place in Northlands Park as part of Edmonton's Klondike Days, was a theatrical and musical tribute to Alberta's soldiers and police officers of the past century. 3. The Celebrate Canada Centennial Jam at Edmonton's Commonwealth Stadium featured talent from across Canada. 4. Bagpipers lend their sound to celebrations at Métis Crossing.

Opposite: 1. A young Edmontonian takes part in the city's New Year's Eve 2005 celebrations honouring Alberta's Centennial. 2. Alberta Centennial Ambassador Dorothy French takes a wagon ride as part of Millet's celebrations. 3. Gary Mar, Community Development Minister, presents tickets to the Centennial Kick-off Party to military personnel and their families in recognition of their contributions to Alberta and Canada. 4. Albertans everywhere waved the flag for Alberta's Centennial.

This page: The Calgary Stampede embraced Alberta's Centennial with traditional western enthusiasm.

Opposite: Edmonton's Klondike Days parade took on a Centennial theme.

Celebrate Alberta!

Two teams of high school drama students hit the road during the summer to bring Alberta's history to life at more than 40 community events across the province. Using only funny hats, a plywood time machine and their irrepressible wit, the Celebrate Alberta teams brought smiles to everyone's faces. They marched in local parades, entertained audiences with historical skits, teased them with Alberta trivia quizzes, and rewarded them with Centennial souvenirs.

"We had an amazing audience, all of whom were enjoying what the 'mad scientist' had to show them. I would like to thank Vegreville for having delicious perogies for us between shows and for knowing how to put on a great closing show with fiddlers and dancers!"
CELEBRATE ALBERTA TEAM MEMBER JILL FUSCO
AT VEGREVILLE'S UKRAINIAN PYSANKA FESTIVAL

"Hail - that's right, hail. We were pelted. But, it didn't seem to stop the rodeo, so we didn't let it stop us. We immediately set out to perform what could be the most fun part of our job: handing out the free stuff! The spectators were more than happy to answer our questions and received some cool stuff and good times in the process. We did two big shows and were surprised by the knowledge our audience members possessed. Seriously impressive, go Airdrie!"
CELEBRATE ALBERTA TEAM MEMBER ALEX KINGCOTT
AT THE AIRDRIE PRO RODEO

"From the model airplanes, to the Skyhawk parachute jumpers, and an appearance from Canada's very own Snowbirds, this show had it all including delicious pitas and inflatable swords. Our show was packed with enthusiastic audience members and, of course, crazy dancing."

CELEBRATE ALBERTA TEAM MEMBER MATTHEW BOWEN
AT THE GRANDE PRAIRIE CENTENNIAL AIR SHOW / STREET PERFORMERS FESTIVAL

"We had bleachers right in front of where we set up. When people got tired they would come to rest and we would suck them into our time-travelling world of wonder. The audience was really great. We had leftover prizes to give away so after all the trivia was done we had 'crazy dancing' and 'yell-as-loud-as-you-can' contests. Overall it was a super performance in a super town."

CELEBRATE ALBERTA TEAM MEMBER MEGAN MACDONALD
AT COALDALE SETTLERS DAYS

This page and opposite: Celebrate Alberta team members add a quirky layer of fun to Centennial celebrations in communities around the province.

Reliving history

Museums, historic sites, cultural facilities and provincial parks across the province took visitors on a romp through the past. Many mounted special exhibitions and events highlighting significant developments in Alberta's history.

The Royal Alberta Museum revisited a century of special occasions in Alberta with its *Alberta Celebrates* Centennial exhibition. The Glenbow Museum weighed in with the launch of its new *Mavericks: An Incorrigible History of Alberta* gallery.

Mavericks will trace the history of Alberta from its first people to the present and explore what it means to be an Albertan.

Lieutenant Governor Norman Kwong hosted a 1905-themed garden party on the grounds of Government House and the Royal Alberta Museum on the Sunday following the September 1 Centennial celebrations. Guests dressed in period clothing. Families enjoyed old fashioned fun including a marching band, rag-time piano, Chinese lion dance, lemonade, popcorn and birthday cake.

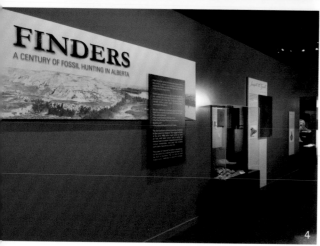

강원정

Opposite: 1. Summer visitors to the Alberta Legislature found tour guides dressed in 1905 period costumes. 2. Visitors to Cypress Hills Provincial Park during *History in the Hills 2005 – A Centennial Celebration* enjoyed music, performances, demonstrations and stories from the Blackfoot, Cree, Nakoda and Métis traditions. 3. Period costumes were seen at the 1905-themed garden party hosted by Lieutenant Governor Norman Kwong on the grounds of Government House and the Royal Alberta Museum. 4. The Royal Tyrrell Museum's exhibition *Finders: A Century of Fossil Hunting in Alberta* relived discoveries by palaeontologists in Alberta's badlands from the late 1800s to the present.

This page: 1. Premier Ralph Klein (l.) and representatives of Gangwon, Alberta's sister province, at the dedication of the Korean pavilion on the grounds of the Royal Alberta Museum. The pavilion was a Centennial gift from Gangwon. 2 & 3: The Royal Alberta Museum mounted *Hoof Prints to Tank Tracks – 100 Years of the South Alberta Light Horse* and *Queens of the Court: The Edmonton Grads,* featuring the "winningest" team of any sport, at any time, in Canada.

HOOF PRINTS
TO TANK TRACKS
100 Years of the South Alberta Light Horse
Alberta's Regiment
1905 - 2005

CANADA

Doris N
GUAR

3

Making the Centennial their business

Countless businesses and non-profit organizations incorporated Centennial themes into their activities and annual events for 2005. One example was Shell Canada's *Spirit of the Future Awards,* which provided each of 30 young people aged 16 to 25 with a $5,000 scholarship and a $5,000 donation to the winner's designated not-for-profit organization. Winners were also featured in vignettes on Global Television's network.

1. Employees of GWL Realty Advisors Inc. created a landscaping display for the company's Alberta Environment tenants in the Forestry Building commemorating the people of Alberta who helped develop the province's natural resources.
2. Alberta-grown ATCO Group of Companies showed itself a "pioneer of Alberta spirit" by sending a travelling exhibit, *Places in Time,* to 53 communities across the province.
3. Save On Foods ran a major Alberta Centennial promotion, making 2005 Centennial flags available at its stores throughout the province and running a Centennial Bash "Scan and Win" contest offering cars, trips and other prizes. 4. United Farmers of Alberta hit the road with *Our History in Motion,* a travelling caravan commemorating a century of co-operative service to agriculture in Alberta.

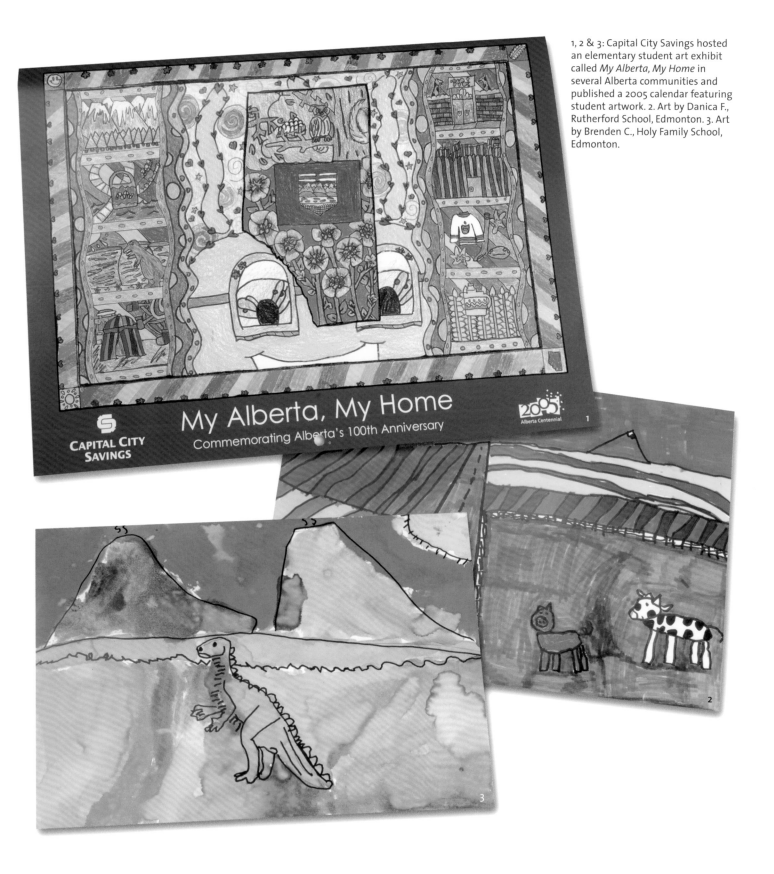

1, 2 & 3: Capital City Savings hosted an elementary student art exhibit called *My Alberta, My Home* in several Alberta communities and published a 2005 calendar featuring student artwork. 2. Art by Danica F., Rutherford School, Edmonton. 3. Art by Brenden C., Holy Family School, Edmonton.

My Alberta, My Home
Commemorating Alberta's 100th Anniversary

CAPITAL CITY
SAVINGS

2005
Alberta Centennial

Sporting their Centennial colours

Albertans love their sports and 2005 gave them even more to cheer about.

The 2005 World Masters Games, the largest multi-sport games in the world, were held in Edmonton in recognition of the Centennial. The event attracted 21,285 athletes from 84 countries. Also in Edmonton, some of the world's fastest runners laced up their shoes for the IAAF World Half Marathon Championships.

Canmore hosted special Centennial celebrations in conjunction with the Alberta Centennial World Cup of cross-country skiing. Alberta athletes, including Becky Scott and Sara Renner, had their best results ever in a world cup race.

The 2005 Tim Hortons Brier took to the ice at Rexall Place in Edmonton. The Brier established the Alberta Curling Athletes of the Century program recognizing Alberta's top curlers and teams of the past 100 years. Randy Ferbey was named Alberta's Curler of the Century, and Ferbey's foursome, Alberta's Curling Team of the Century.

Alberta's two Canadian Football League teams — the Edmonton Eskimos and the Calgary Stampeders — celebrated year-round by wearing Alberta 2005 Centennial crests on their jerseys. Alberta's minor football teams also wore Centennial logos. Other Centennial promotions included the halftime shows at the Labour Day Classic and Rematch Games in 2004 and 2005 between the Edmonton Eskimos and Calgary Stampeders.

Going to extremes

Some Albertans went to great lengths and heights to celebrate Alberta's 100th birthday with a degree of symbolism. Canadian Forces Base Suffield opened the gates of the national wildlife area within the base boundaries to host the Alberta Centennial Trail Ride. Some 850 riders saddled up and travelled a 100-kilometre loop to get a taste of life 100 years ago on the pristine prairies.

Members of the Alberta Centennial Mountain Expedition marked the Centennial by summiting 100 peaks in Alberta's Rocky Mountains. The expedition, nicknamed "The Century", was sponsored in part by The Royal Canadian Geographical Society.

5

6

4

Opposite and this page: 1. Team Ferbey was named Alberta's Curling Team of the Century at the 2005 Tim Hortons Brier. 2. Beckie Scott crosses the finish line to win the Gold Medal in the Women's 15km Classic race at the Alberta Centennial World Cup. 3 & 4: The Calgary Stampeders and Edmonton Eskimos wore 2005 Centennial crests year-round. 5. Hundreds of volunteers participated in an attempt to climb 100 summits in the Alberta Rockies throughout the summer of 2005. 6. Participants in the Alberta Centennial Trail Ride got a taste of life 100 years ago on the prairies.

Celebrating Alberta's Aboriginal peoples

The Aboriginal peoples of Alberta took pride in celebrating their role in the province's history and development. First Nation and Métis communities held special events and incorporated Alberta's Centennial into their annual festivals and Pow Wows. National Aboriginal Day events across the province in June commemorated Alberta's Centennial and the province's first residents.

The Métis Nation of Alberta staged the Métis Crossing Centennial Voyage, retracing the route taken by Métis voyageurs along the North Saskatchewan River from Fort Edmonton to Métis Crossing, near Smoky Lake. Centennial voyageurs spent three days paddling, camping, and sharing stories about Métis history and culture. Approximately 2,000 people including Métis from across Alberta, Saskatchewan and Manitoba greeted the arrival of the canoes at Métis Crossing.

The Athabasca Chipewyan First Nation hosted the K'ai Taile Denesuline Gathering celebrating Denesuline customs, culture, and traditions through activities such as canoe races, moose hide tanning demonstrations and stories told by elders.

1. Eating and sharing bannock was part of Centennial celebrations in Alberta's Métis communities. 2. National Aboriginal Day celebrations at Heritage Park in Fort McMurray featured traditional dances.

A Métis hunting and trapping tent (l.) and three First Nation tipis provide opportunities for people to experience and explore Aboriginal culture and history during Alberta's Centennial year.

1 & 3: Participants and organizers of the Métis Crossing Centennial Voyage, an event retracing the voyageur route from Fort Edmonton to Métis Crossing near Smoky Lake.
2. People of all ages participated in Centennial celebrations in Aboriginal communities throughout the province.

National Aboriginal Day 2005 celebrations at Heritage Park in Fort McMurray.

A dancer from the Siksika Nation performs at a stop along the 2005 Calgary Stampede Trail Ride carried out in celebration of Alberta's Centennial. Riders trailed bucking horses from the Stampede Ranch in Hanna to Stampede Park.

Taking the arts to the people

Alberta's artists hit the road, taking their music, words and art to communities around the province. A bus filled with Alberta performers rolled into 10 communities as part of a special concert series presented by the Government of Alberta. *Alberta Tracks: A Centennial Music Celebration* showcased the talents of 30 musicians and groups in free concerts attended by more than 2,000 people.

The Writers Guild of Alberta celebrated the province's Centennial and its own 25th anniversary by sending 100 writers to 100 communities to present readings and workshops. The guild staged *Write Around Alberta* to "show our appreciation for people who have shared their words and to those who give us new words."

The Alberta Society of Artists toured a juried show *Memory and Identity* celebrating Alberta's Centennial and its own 75th anniversary. In Alberta's largest choral concert and tour ever, over 400 singers and 11 conductors from Edmonton, Calgary and Lethbridge performed in each of the three cities.

One enterprising country and western singer, Matt Masters, performed 100 gigs singing 100 Alberta-related songs around the province.

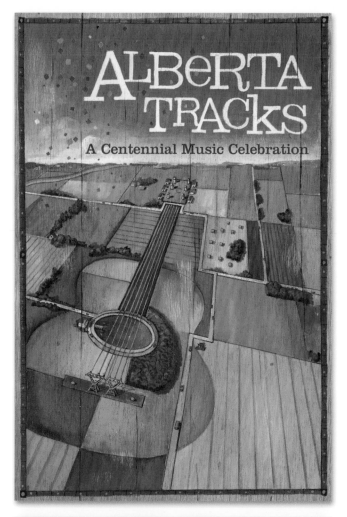

Alberta Tracks entertainers 1. Wil; 2. Maria Dunn; and 3. The Swiftys.

Looking back with the next generation

Children and youth across Alberta took a fresh look at Alberta's history and future as they threw themselves into creative projects in schools across the province. Alberta Education's Centennial School History Project invited students in Grades K-12 to tell the story of their schools through words, video, music, pictures, art, dance, or multimedia. Imagination was the only limit for young people participating in *If Walls Could Speak....*

In another Centennial project, Alberta Education called on students in Grades 4, 5, and 6 to participate in *Song Writing Intensive*. Groups of students in eight schools selected through winning essays honed their song-writing skills in workshops with Mary Kieftenbeld, writer of Alberta's official song. The students wrote songs about their own school or community and invited friends and neighbours to hear them perform their compositions.

In some of countless other school Centennial projects: Ponoka Composite High School students created a Centennial mural with a local artist.

Springfield Elementary School in Peace River held a Family Reading Night featuring fresh-made bannock, a round dance, and Alberta birthday cake.

Grades 1 and 2 students at the Champion Community School wished 100 wishes for the babies born in 2005 in the Champion/Carmangay areas and read their wishes to a group of new moms and babies.

Students at Busby School, in the Pembina Hills Regional Division, transformed their entire school into a museum, complete with a tipi, fort, pioneer home and papier-mâché bison in the hallways.

Holy Cross Collegiate students in Strathmore staged the "Great Capital Debate" of 1906, portraying historical figures who debated where Alberta's seat of government should be. The event included a typical 1906 meal.

Top: A page from *Looking Back,* a PowerPoint presentation with a "magic scrapbook" created by the Grade 5 class at Beiseker Community School for Alberta Education's *If Walls Could Speak...* Centennial project. Bottom: A scrapbook of memories put together by students in Grades K-6 at Midway School in Didsbury.

3: Students of Suzuki Charter School in Edmonton painted a whimsical mural depicting the school's [pas]sionate focus on music. Fittingly, one of the school's ensemble groups played music at the unveiling of [the] mural. 2. Students at Allan Johnstone School in Hardisty take part in Alberta Education's *Song Writing* [Inte]*nsive* with musician Chris Andrews.

"Grade 5 students at MacKenzie Lake Elementary School presented eight skits portraying every aspect of Alberta's citizens, industries and pioneer spirit. The variety of skits, enthusiasm of each student and the sincere efforts of the teachers was very evident. At the conclusion of the program, the Alberta Centennial Song was sung and to see each student singing this song brought tears to my eyes. I wish that all citizens of Alberta could be as proud of their province as these young students."

BRYCE NIMMO, CENTENNIAL AMBASSADOR, CALGARY

River Valley School – *Tip Your Hat*

Verse 1:
At the foothills of the Rockies
On the banks of the old red deer
Sits a little town called Sundre
Full of beauty through the year
Verse 2:
Cowboy trail winds through town
With cowpokes herdin' cattle
On horseback in the mountains
Sittin' high upon their saddle
Chorus:
We're building a better future
It's beautiful and bright
On the wings of our eagle
Our minds have taken flight
And we'll try as hard as we can
To make our mural grand
Getting friends to join us
And lend a helping hand
At the River Valley School
At the River Valley School
Verse 3:
With the changing of the seasons
The little creek has froze
She begins to break-up
When that old chinook wind blows
Verse 4:
Cowboys and trick riders
Bucking broncos star in June
Mutton bustin', barrel racin'
Tip your hat and come back soon
Chorus

Written on November 2, 2005 by Grades 4-6 students at River Valley School, Sundre with Mary Kieftenbeld and John Wort Hannam as part of the Alberta Education Centennial project Song Writing Intensive.

A Celebration Fit for a Queen

Albertans were delighted to welcome Her Majesty Queen Elizabeth II and His Royal Highness the Duke of Edinburgh to their party in May. The action-packed three-day Royal Visit, May 23-25, included an historic visit to the Alberta Legislature and several special Centennial events in Edmonton and Calgary.

In honour of Her Majesty's visit, the Provincial Museum of Alberta was renamed the Royal Alberta Museum. Highway 2 between Edmonton and Calgary, Alberta's most travelled highway, also received a new name: the Queen Elizabeth II Highway. The Government of Alberta launched the Queen Elizabeth II Graduate Scholarship Program to reward the achievements of students pursuing graduate studies in Alberta.

Singing in the rain

The Queen was the guest of honour for the Centennial Kick-off at Edmonton's Commonwealth Stadium marking 100 days until Alberta's September 1 birthday. More than 25,000 hardy Albertans huddled under tarps and umbrellas, refusing to let the rainy weather spoil their fun, while more than 1,500 dancers, musicians and cultural entertainers helped lift everyone's spirits.

The Royal Couple joined the crowd in watching performances by Alberta artists including Michael Carey, Senator Tommy Banks, Jens Lindemann, the Black Pioneer Heritage Singers and the White Buffalo Dancers and Drummers. As a finale, Ian Tyson sang his famous Alberta anthem *Four Strong Winds* with backup from the singers and other artists unable to perform due to the rain.

Royal Visit
ALBERTA CENTENNIAL
2005

Her Majesty Queen Elizabeth II
Queen of Canada
and
His Royal Highness
The Duke of Edinburgh

Alberta
May 23 - 25, 2005

Alberta · Alberta Centennial

Opposite: The Queen takes part in a cake-cutting ceremony with Premier Ralph Klein, signaling the beginning of Alberta's 100th birthday celebrations, while the crowd sings *Happy Birthday*.

This page: 1, 3, 4: Some of the thousands of Albertans who braved the rain to welcome the Queen at Commonwealth Stadium. 2. The Guard of Honour enters the stadium.

This page and opposite: Pipes and red serge added colour to the pageantry honouring the Queen at Commonwealth Stadium.

"When she smiles, the world lights up.
Her smile is so warm and friendly."

<small>OVERHEARD DURING THE ROYAL VISIT</small>

Opposite: 1. The Queen inspects the Guard of Honour. 2. The White Buffalo Dancers and Drummers perform for the Queen. 3 & 4: Smiles from Her Majesty charm the crowd.

This page: 1. The Mounted Troop of Lord Strathcona Horse were part of the pageantry at Commonwealth Stadium. 2. Lieutenant Governor Norman Kwong, Her Majesty Queen Elizabeth II, and Premier Klein at the welcoming ceremonies in Commonwealth Stadium. 3 & 4: Everybody and his dog were determined not to let the rain spoil their day. 5. Michael Carey sings Alberta's official song.

"Although the rain never let up, the weather failed to dampen our spirits. While we waited patiently under our rain ponchos to meet the Queen we sang the quintessential rain song, Singing in the Rain, which turned into a stereo rendition when the RCMP musical band joined in. The warm feeling of camaraderie and good will is something I will always remember about the day."

AUDREY LUFT, CENTENNIAL AMBASSADOR, EDMONTON

"Whenever I hear the song Singing in the Rain it will conjure up the image of going to meet the Queen at Commonwealth Stadium wearing a baggy."

RITA THOMPSON, CENTENNIAL AMBASSADOR, OLDS

Conducting Royal business

The Queen toured the Provincial Museum of Alberta and participated in a ceremony renaming it the Royal Alberta Museum. Meanwhile, the Duke of Edinburgh visited Fort McMurray for a close-up look at Alberta's oil sands. Later, the Queen visited the Legislature Building and in an historic speech became the first reigning monarch to address the Alberta Legislative Assembly.

Opposite: 1, 2, 4: The Queen greets Albertans during a walkabout on the grounds of the Royal Alberta Museum and Government House, accompanied by Premier Ralph Klein (1) and Lieutenant Governor Norman Kwong (4). 3. Tracey Gladue (in hard hat), a heavy equipment operator at Suncor Energy, gives Prince Phillip (second from left) a tour of her Cat 797 heavy hauler.

This page: 1. A mural celebrating Alberta and Saskatchewan's Centennials parts as the Queen prepares to enter the Royal Alberta Museum. 2. The Queen and Premier Klein unveil a plaque in the renaming ceremony for the museum as museum director Bruce McGillivray (r.) and Mrs. Colleen Klein look on.

"We're very proud. She is the Queen. We are her loyal subjects, her soldiers. She's a lovely lady."

Opposite: 1. At the Legislature, the Queen unveiled a set of stained glass windows highlighting the role of the monarchy in Alberta over the past 100 years. 2. Loyal veterans pay respects to their Queen. 3. The Queen stops to chat with fellow Corgi-fanciers during a walkabout on the Legislature grounds. 4. The Queen enters the Legislature, where she will become the first reigning monarch to address the Alberta Legislative Assembly.

This page: 1. The Queen starts her walkabout on the Legislature grounds. 2. The Queen and Premier Klein greet guests at a dinner hosted by the Government of Alberta in Edmonton. 3. Premier Klein unveils a plaque commemorating the renaming of Highway 2 the Queen Elizabeth II Highway.

Circling the Square in Edmonton

Edmonton Mayor Stephen Mandel and Edmonton City Council welcomed the Queen and the Duke of Edinburgh to City Hall on their final day in Edmonton. During a walkabout in Sir Winston Churchill Square, the Royal Couple charmed an adoring crowd of about 10,000. Her Majesty presented Queen's Centennial Bursaries to 35 Grade 12 students, one from every Edmonton high school.

Opposite: Edmonton Mayor Stephen Mandel accompanies the Queen during a walkabout in Sir Winston Churchill Square.

This page: Prince Phillip shares a laugh with the crowd in Sir Winston Churchill Square.

Calgary rolls out the welcome mat

Calgarians displayed their characteristic western hospitality as they hosted the conclusion to the Royal Visit. On arriving in Calgary, the Queen and Prince Phillip had a private tour of the Museum of the Regiments. The Royal Couple then attended a luncheon for 1,000 at the Round-Up Centre hosted by Premier Klein. A spirited farewell program at the Pengrowth Saddledome and 21-gun salute provided a fitting finale to a most memorable Royal Visit.

1. Premier Klein chats with children eagerly waiting to see the Queen.
2 & 4: Crowds line the streets of Calgary to extend a warm welcome as the Queen's motorcade passes. 3. The Queen poses for photos with officers of Her Majesty's Canadian regiments during a special visit to the Museum of the Regiments.

"This is a great day. We should remember it forever. It gives you chills just being here."

OVERHEARD AT THE QUEEN'S OFFICIAL FAREWELL PROGRAM

A spirited farewell at the Saddledome

A crowd of 17,000 packed the Pengrowth Saddledome to the rafters to experience the pageantry of the Queen's official farewell to Alberta and Canada. The spectacular program, hosted by the City of Calgary, highlighted Calgary's western roots and closed with the entrance of the Guard of Honour, Royal inspection and a 21-gun salute.

1, 3, 4: Entertainers at the Queen's official farewell program highlighted Calgary's multiculturalism and western roots. 2. The program closed with the entrance of the Guard of Honour and Royal inspection.

"It was a very humbling experience and something I will cherish for the rest of my life. She was a very easy person to speak to."

Calgary Mayor Dave Bronconnier

"I'm always going to remember her smile. She has a really nice smile."

<small>OVERHEARD DURING THE QUEEN'S VISIT TO CALGARY</small>

Farewell and come back again soon!

The Party of the Century

It was a party for the record books. More than 250,000 Albertans joined together to celebrate the province's official birthday on September 1, making it the biggest party in Alberta's history. They partied all day and into the night, enjoying family fun, birthday cake and entertainment by the finest home-grown Alberta talent. Provincial parks offered free camping while provincial museums and historic sites offered free admission in honour of the occasion.

"*The faces of children... enjoying this once-in-a-lifetime event reminded me of the spirit of community pride and friendship that pervaded the country dances and events in small town Alberta years ago. I like to think that we created memories in the minds of our youth that night that will make them proud of our past and proud Albertans into the future.*"

WILLIAM HULL, CENTENNIAL AMBASSADOR, RED DEER

AlbertaSpirit kicks off

Ten communities across the province hosted official AlbertaSpirit parties, each with its own unique flavour and headliner artists. They included: Edmonton, Calgary, Banff, Bonnyville, Fort McMurray, Grande Prairie, Lethbridge, Medicine Hat, Red Deer and Wainwright. The communities were selected so that the maximum number of Albertans could join the fun within a reasonable driving distance from home. Crowds in each location watched live performances from other AlbertaSpirit communities on massive jumbotrons, making it a truly province-wide party.

Those who couldn't make it watched the festivities live on television or on the Internet.

In the evening, star-studded gala concerts showed off the newly renovated Jubilee Auditoria in Edmonton and Calgary and entertained the crowd at the Legislature grounds. The celebration of the century culminated in ooohs and aaahs as simultaneous fireworks lit up the skies in the 10 AlbertaSpirit communities.

Edmonton

Alberta's birthday party got off to a hearty start in the capital city with a free pancake breakfast hosted by the City of Edmonton. Volunteers from the Ismaili Muslim community and public officials from all orders of government served flap jacks to over 8,000 guests at the Capital "E" Centennial Breakfast in Sir Winston Churchill Square.

A virtual birthday party

After flipping pancakes at the Centennial Breakfast, Premier Ralph Klein dashed over to the Victoria School of Performing and Visual Arts to connect with students from around the province via the SuperNet for a virtual birthday party. Students at the Victoria School, Summitview Elementary School in Grande Cache, Schuler Elementary in Schuler, and Mother Teresa Catholic School in Sylvan Lake shared their vision of Alberta with the Premier and Education Minister Gene Zwozdesky. They ate birthday cake, sang *Happy Birthday,* and took in a history lesson via video conference with scientists from the Royal Tyrrell Museum. Bell Canada and Axia partnered with Alberta Education to connect the virtual party-goers.

Opposite: 1. Premier Ralph Klein, and students and teachers at Victoria School of Performing and Visual Arts, share a virtual birthday party via SuperNet with students at schools around the province. 2. L. to r: Edmonton Mayor Stephen Mandel, Deputy Prime Minister Anne McLellan, Mrs. Colleen Klein and Premier Ralph Klein cut birthday cake at the Capital "E" Centennial Breakfast. 3. Premier Klein (centre) receives a pancake flipping tip. 4. Deputy Prime Minister Anne McLellan serves one of the 8,000 guests who turned out at the breakfast. 5. Education Minister Gene Zwozdesky shows off his pancake-flipping style.

This page: 1, 2 & 3: The Alberta Centennial Time Capsule and thousands of Edmonton area residents started the big day at the Capital "E" Centennial Breakfast in Sir Winston Churchill Square before moving to the Legislature grounds for the official Centennial celebrations.

AlbertaSpirit takes flight

Tens of thousands of Albertans streamed onto the Legislature grounds to be part of history as Premier Ralph Klein, joined by Governor General Adrienne Clarkson, Prime Minister Paul Martin, and Lieutenant Governor Norman Kwong, officially launched the AlbertaSpirit celebrations. The Royal Canadian Artillery Band added to the pageantry of the day.

2. Community Development Minister Gary Mar, whose department was responsible for Alberta's Centennial celebrations, greets the crowd at the Legislature grounds. 3. Governor General Adrienne Clarkson and her husband John Ralston Saul arrive at the Legislature grounds.

Becoming a province, déjà vu?

Highlights of the afternoon at the Legislature included an entertaining re-enactment of Alberta's 1905 inauguration ceremony. Local actors played famous Albertans from the past. Alberta's world champion figure skater Kurt Browning was master of ceremonies for the celebrations. Free birthday cake, military and historical displays, a children's area with face painting, a food fair, and family entertainment — including the fleet-footed Shumka Dancers and the Kupalo Ukrainian Dancers, the polka tunes of The Emeralds, the fantastic fiddling of Barrage, and the country sounds of Adam Gregory — rounded out the fun.

Opposite: 1, 2, 3, 5: Performers in period costumes presented a re-enactment of Alberta's 1905 inaugural ceremonies and later mingled with the crowd at the Legislature Building. 4. The official launch of the AlbertaSpirit celebrations took place on a stage designed to depict the pageantry of the 1905 inauguration. At centre stage (l. to r.): Prime Minister Paul Martin, Mrs. Mary Kwong and Lieutenant Governor Norman Kwong, Governor General Adrienne Clarkson and John Ralston Saul, Mrs. Colleen Klein and Premier Ralph Klein.

This page: 1. The Kupalo Ukrainian Dancers. 2. Adam Gregory 3. Barrage 4. The Emeralds.

98

Calgary

Calgary's Brilliant City Festival and a United Way Parade in honour of Alberta's Centennial filled the Olympic Plaza Cultural District with fun, frivolity and festive red balloons. The event featured musical entertainment and a riot of street performers from magicians to breakdancers and a silver Elvis. Crowds followed the EPCOR Centre for the Performing Arts' roving play *Sandstone Cowboys* and bellied up to a massive 100-foot birthday cake. Evening festivities were hosted by Karen Percy-Lowe.

Prime Minister Paul Martin, Premier Ralph Klein and Calgary Mayor Dave Bronconnier cut into Calgary's 100-foot birthday cake.

4

2

3

1. Karen Percy-Lowe and Premier Ralph Klein, in Calgary, press the button starting simultaneous fireworks across the province.

Banff

With the scenic Rocky Mountains as a backdrop, crowds in Banff's Central Park enjoyed great entertainment from local favourites and headliner Maren Ord, a community barbecue, and fun and games for all. As the sun set, the evening sparkled with fireflies – a warm-up to the stunning fireworks that lit up the mountains later in the night.

2. Banff headliner Maren Ord.

"Standing with 1,000 community members and my immediate family around me watching the magnificent fireworks light up the Bow River and the mountains... It was a moment I felt blessed to be Canadian, blessed to be an Albertan and so blessed to call Banff my home."

KAREN SORENSEN, CENTENNIAL AMBASSADOR, BANFF

112

Bonnyville

The Centennial celebrations at the Bonnyville Rodeo Grounds brought together 8,000 residents from the communities of Bonnyville, Cold Lake, Glendon and the M.D. of Bonnyville. Party-goers filled up on free burgers and hot dogs plus regional favourites including pyrogies and bannock. Popular local entertainers – including Clayton Bellamy, Brett Kissel and Daniel Gervais – kept the crowd in good spirits until fireworks topped off a perfect day.

Fort McMurray

Fort McMurray hosted a "Picnic on the Island" at MacDonald Island Park in a double-barreled event to kick off its famous Blueberry Festival and celebrate Alberta's Centennial.

The country fair atmosphere featured carnival rides, a farmers market and performances by home-grown talent including country music star Aaron Lines.

2. Party-goers in Fort McMurray's MacDonald Island Park catch Paul Brandt's performance at the gala in Edmonton's Northern Alberta Jubilee Auditorium via a huge jumbotron.

2. Country music star Aaron Lines.

Grande Prairie

A grand time was had by all at Grande Prairie's AlbertaSpirit birthday carnival, held at Centre 2000. There was dancing, singing, and plenty of cake, plus great entertainment topped by headliners Wide Mouth Mason.

2. L. to r: Fairview Centennial Ambassador Larry Chorney; Mel Knight, MLA, Grande Prairie-Smoky; Grande Prairie Centennial Ambassadors Perky McCullough and Patricia Reid; Minister of Gaming Gordon Graydon, MLA, Grande Prairie-Wapiti; and Grande Prairie Mayor Wayne Ayling. Ms. McCullough holds Grande Prairie's micro time capsule, which would later be deposited in the Alberta Centennial Time Capsule for future Albertans to discover.

1. A singer with Wide Mouth Mason entertains at the AlbertaSpirit party in Grande Prairie beside a jumbotron showing live entertainment from other AlbertaSpirit communities.

Lethbridge

Lethbridge rocked with a musical extravaganza by New West Theatre at Exhibition Park. Then the crowd moseyed on over to Henderson Lake Park for a stunning fireworks display amplified by reflections on the surface of the lake.

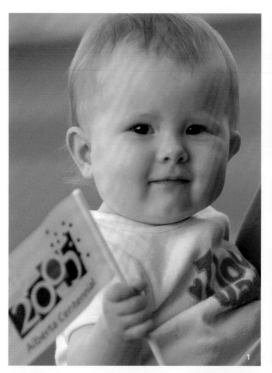

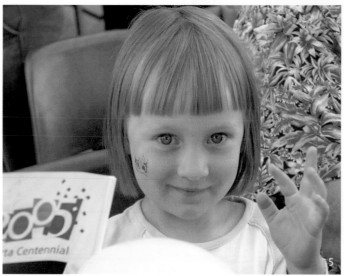

"I mostly like them all, but maybe I like the ones that sound like popcorn best. No! Maybe I like the sparkles best. Oh! I like the ones that are just red!"

A YOUNG ALBERTAN'S COMMENTARY ON THE ALBERTASPIRIT FIREWORKS DISPLAY

Medicine Hat

Hatters celebrated their own unique history by hosting their Centennial party at the Clay Industries National Historic District. Celebrations included a line-up of local talent and tours of the Medalta Potteries museum.

Red Deer

Red Deer hosted what had to be the "coolest" festivities of the day with hockey and figure skating demonstrations on the ice at Westerner Park. Olympic Gold Medal figure skaters Jamie Salé and David Pelletier hosted an action-packed evening of entertainment including popular country music star Danny Hooper.

1. Danny Hooper.

"Our most significant memory occurred when we participated in the Red Deer parade and hosted the evening celebrations. We had an opportunity to meet so many wonderful nurses and veterans who not only served in the great wars for Canada but who were responsible for building our province to what it is today. Meeting them and hearing their stories was very special for both of us. Thank you, Alberta."

JAMIE SALÉ AND DAVID PELLETIER, CENTENNIAL AMBASSADORS, RED DEER

1. Alberta's Olympic Gold Medal pairs figure skater Jamie Salé at Red Deer's AlbertaSpirit celebration.

1

2

3

7

4

6

5

3. Michael Carey performs at Red Deer's AlbertaSpirit celebration.

Wainwright

Wainwright's Centennial celebration at Wallace Park literally took the cake. Dozens of locals rolled up their sleeves and baked a massive cake in the shape of Alberta. The rest of the community did their best to eat it while tapping their feet to the quirky country sounds of Alberta's own Corb Lund Band.

"Wainwright put on a hell of a party."

CORB LUND

2. Headliner Corb Lund helps Wainwright put on "a hell of a party."

Jubilation!

Gala concerts at the newly renovated Jubilee Auditoria on the evening of September 1 featured stellar performances by the cream of Alberta talent. Tickets to the free concerts were distributed through Ticketmaster on a first-come, first-served basis and were snapped up within a day. Spectators thrilled to Tom Jackson's rendition of the Aboriginal performance of *Water, Wind and Fire,* while k.d. lang moved audiences with her electrifying version of Leonard Cohen's *Hallelujah.* Paul Brandt stirred their pride singing *Alberta Bound* to a backdrop of classic Alberta scenery.

1. Bobby Curtola gets the audience rocking at the Legislature grounds. 2. Master of ceremonies Kurt Browning rocks along with the crowd.

Other headliners included Jann Arden, Ian Tyson, Rebecca Jenkins, the Alberta Centennial Jazz Band directed by George Blondheim, the Calgary Philharmonic Orchestra, and a host of Alberta's top musical and dance ensembles.

Kurt Browning hosted more gala entertainment from the Legislature grounds in Edmonton. The crowd rocked and rolled with Bobby Curtola and tapped their feet to Barrage. Party-goers in the AlbertaSpirit host communities eavesdropped on the galas and each other's festivities via jumbotrons throughout the evening. Albertans across the province caught the highlights live on television and the Internet.

1 & 2: Guests at the Jubilee Auditoria galas.
3. L. to r: Lieutenant Governor Norman Kwong, his wife Mary Kwong, Lynn Mandel and Edmonton Mayor Stephen Mandel at the Northern Alberta Jubilee Auditorium AlbertaSpirit gala. 4. Lieutenant Governor Norman Kwong speaks at the gala. 5. Volunteers at the AlbertaSpirit gala. 6. Sound preparations for the gala performances.

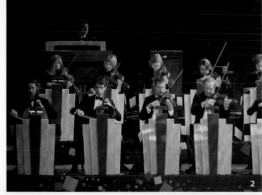

This page: 1. P.J. Perry. 2. The Alberta Centennial Jazz Band. 3 & 4: Paul Brandt. 5. Gala hosts Paul Mennier and Jennifer Martin.

Opposite: 1. k.d. lang sings *Hallelujah*. 2. Tom Jackson performs in *Water, Wind and Fire*. 3. Jann Arden. 4. Ian Tyson.

A bang-up ending

Premier Ralph Klein capped a perfect day in Calgary's Olympic Plaza with the push of a button setting off simultaneous fireworks in AlbertaSpirit host cities across the province. The spectacular pyrotechnics were set to live music, *Alberta Strong and Free,* composed for the occasion by George Blondheim and Bernard Zolner and performed by the Calgary Philharmonic Orchestra and the Alberta Centennial Jazz Band. The fireworks displays included Alberta's trademark wild rose and blue sky cascading over yellow canola fields.

1. The Calgary Philharmonic Orchestra. 2 & 4: Ethnofusion. 3. Alberta Ballet.

Finale at the AlbertaSpirit gala: the Alberta Centennial Jazz Band conducted by George Blondheim and vocalists Thomas Alexander, Jeanetta Jamerson, Sierra Jamerson, Rosalind Harper, and Linda Campbell.

Spreading the Joy

What fun's a party if you don't spread the joy? Albertans found lots of creative ways to share their high spirits with other Canadians and people beyond our borders.

A huge delegation of Alberta's artists threw a 13-day extravaganza in the nation's capital showcasing the finest of Alberta arts and culture. Choristers representing Alberta's Francophone community toured Québec. The Government of Alberta presented the National Gallery of Canada with a gift of Alberta art and created Centennial scholarships for students across Canada. Premier Klein put a special Centennial spin on the annual Council of the Federation summer meeting, extending a warm western welcome to his fellow Canadian premiers.

Making the scene in Ottawa

More than 600 Alberta artists took over Ottawa's arts and culture scene between April 28 and May 10 in the biggest showcase ever of Alberta talent outside the province. Alberta Scene featured 95 events and 315 performances and concerts in 25 venues around the nation's capital. Over 56,000 people attended the performances, garnering national media attention.

The 13-day extravaganza gave audience members a first-hand look at the vitality and diversity of Alberta theatre, music, dance, film, literature, visual arts — and even culinary arts.

The music alone spanned pop, jazz, rock, country, folk, blues, hip hop, classical, Aboriginal and world. Talent scouts from as far as Australia and Korea joined Canadian and American scouts to book Alberta artists for future tours. The festival was mounted by the National Arts Centre and presented by EPCOR with support from the Alberta government and other sponsors.

In November the National Arts Centre Orchestra honoured Alberta and Saskatchewan's Centennials with a 13-day concert tour of both provinces.

This page and opposite: Among the artists performing at Alberta Scene in Ottawa were 1. Country powerhouse Terri Clark; 3. Francophone music sensation Crystal Plamondon; 4. Blues artist Gordie Johnson; 5. Jazz legend Senator Tommy Banks; and 7. Actor-playwrights Daniel Arnold and Medina Hahn. 2. Alberta Scene opened with a full house and a roaring standing ovation for the all-Alberta opera *Filumena*. 6. Music director Pinchas Zukerman led the National Arts Centre Orchestra on a 13-day concert and education tour of Alberta and Saskatchewan.

"Being a part of Alberta Scene felt a little bit like coming home. There were artists from my home province all around me, sharing their Alberta music and stories in front of new audiences."

Jazz legend Senator Tommy Banks

Canada's National Arts Centre

alberta
scene
albertaine

April 28 to May 10 2005
Alberta comes to the Nation's Capital

albertascene.ca

literature! | dance! | visual arts! | theatre! | music!

4

5

7

6

Extending a warm western welcome

Premiers from across Canada were treated to a celebration of Alberta's entry into confederation at the annual Council of the Federation Conference, hosted by Premier Ralph Klein in Banff in August. The premiers arrived in style on a CP Empress steam train and, along with a busy agenda, enjoyed three days of activities harking back to the turn of the last century. The Northwest Territories presented Premier Klein with the chair that Sir Wilfrid Laurier sat in when he signed Alberta into confederation 100 years ago. The chair now resides in the Royal Alberta Museum.

The Government of Alberta also hosted a Centennial-themed Western Premiers' Conference in Lloydminster in May, welcoming premiers from British Columbia, Saskatchewan, Manitoba, Yukon, Northwest Territories and Nunavut.

"We had a CP Empress steam train and vintage cars take all the premiers and delegates to Banff where they attended all the events done in a turn-of-the-century Centennial theme. The premiers put an official photo and conference program signed by all into the Centennial Time Capsule. The official reception and dinner for 600 was held outdoors along the banks of the Spray River featuring dinners cooked from chuckwagons, campfires, blacksmiths, performances by the Mount Royal Youth Orchestra and Jason McCoy and a recreated ride of the NWMP by the Steele's Scout troop."

JACK DONAHUE, CALGARY, CENTENNIAL AMBASSADOR

Opposite: The Steele's Scout Troop recreates the ride of the North West Mounted Police for guests of the Council of the Federation Conference.

This page: 1. Premiers at the Council of the Federation Conference pose for a photo on the CPR Empress. 2. Premiers and guests are greeted by entertainers in period costume in Banff. 3. Premiers meet the media at a news conference at the end of the Council of the Federation Conference. 4. L to r: International and Intergovernmental Relations Minister Ed Stelmach, Premier Ralph Klein, US Ambassador David Wilkins, and Colin Robertson, Minister and Head of the Washington Advocacy Secretariat, Government of Canada, meet with premiers at the conference.

Gifts of art and knowledge

The Government of Alberta presented a painting by Alberta artist Joane Cardinal-Schubert to the National Gallery of Canada in recognition of the province's Centennial. *Song of My Dreambed Dance* was selected as an expressive symbol of Alberta's proud history and the heritage of its Aboriginal people.

The Province also launched the Alberta Centennial Scholarships Program as a Centennial gift from Alberta to all Canadians. The program will provide 325 scholarships annually to post-secondary students across Canada —25 students from each province and territory, including Alberta.

Including those less fortunate

Albertans' typical generosity of spirit came to the fore often throughout the year. Communities and groups around the province spread their joy by incorporating fundraising for a variety of causes into their Centennial celebrations. One of the most poignant was a spontaneous fundraiser launched by the residents of Lacombe for their twin community of Lacombe, Louisiana, following Hurricane Katrina's devastation.

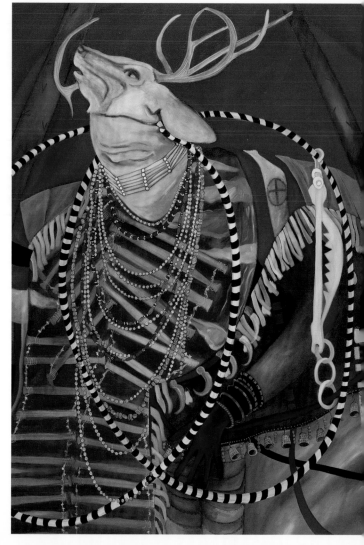

Joane Cardinal-Schubert, *Song of My Dreambed Dance*, 1995.

"My most memorable moment was during our Centennial celebrations in Lacombe September 3. Our guests from our twin community of Lacombe, Louisiana, could not make our party due to Hurricane Katrina. We launched a fundraising campaign to assist them. We had people stuffing money into a water jug. Even the little children came up to me to put their dimes, nickels and pennies into the jug. It was a very touching moment."

BILL McQUESTEN, CENTENNIAL AMBASSADOR, LACOMBE

"When I visited Eastbrook Elementary School in January, I urged the students to use the representative number of 100 in their Centennial activities. The Grade 4 class made a $100 donation to the SPCA. The kids had brought pennies to school and rolled them into lots of 100. When they reached their goal of $100, they chose to donate the money to a charity over having a party. They were all smiles with the pyramid of rolled pennies on the floor in front of them."

JACQUELINE (JACKIE) MURRAY, CENTENNIAL AMBASSADOR, BROOKS

"My most memorable moment was attending the Chorale Saint-Jean, Faculté Saint-Jean, concert in Victoriaville, Québec... In Victoriaville, the choir played to a packed house (including the mayor and many other dignitaries) in the Arthabaska church which Sir Wilfrid Laurier attended while he lived in the region. This was especially significant as Sir Wilfrid Laurier was Prime Minister of Canada when Alberta became a province in 1905."

SENATOR CLAUDETTE TARDIF, CENTENNIAL AMBASSADOR, EDMONTON

Standing ovations in Québec

Chorale Saint-Jean, of the Faculté Saint-Jean, demonstrated the vitality of the Francophone community in Alberta by mounting a 10-day tour of Québec. The choir sang before mostly sell-out crowds and received standing ovations at each stop on their tour.

1. Chorale Saint-Jean appeared at Église Saint-Christophe d'Arthabaska, Victoriaville, Québec, the church attended by Sir Wilfrid Laurier when he lived in the area. 2. Chorale Saint-Jean at *Festival international de l'art vocal de Trois-Rivières*, Trois-Rivières, Québec.

Sharing the Limelight

Alberta wasn't the only centenarian in 2005. Our province's next door neighbour, Saskatchewan, also turned 100. In addition, Alberta shared the limelight with several Alberta communities and a hardy bunch of individuals who celebrated their 100th birthdays in 2005.

A tale of two provinces

Alberta and Saskatchewan marked their shared milestone by engaging in a little friendly rivalry. The provinces joined forces with the Western Hockey League and the City of Lloydminster to hold the Centennial Cup Hockey Challenge in the border city. This special hockey game featured many of the top junior hockey players in the Western Hockey League. The game was broadcast live on CBC and hosted by CBC's Ron MacLean. Team Alberta defeated Team Saskatchewan 7 to 5. Ticket holders received Centennial commemorative T-shirts. The trophy presented to the winners now rests in the Hockey Hall of Fame awaiting the next Centennial Challenge.

Legendary rivals the Edmonton Eskimos and Saskatchewan Roughriders ended their two-game Centennial Gridiron Challenge with a tie. After polling fans, the Eskimos and Roughriders announced their all-century teams.

Edmonton Eskimo All-Century Team

Quarterback:

Warren Moon

Running Backs:

Normie Kwong

Johnny Bright

Offensive Line:

Hector Pothier

Rod Connop

Leo Groenewegen

Blake Dermott

Bruce Beaton

Receivers:

Brian Kelly

Terry Vaughn

Tom Scott

Jason Tucker

Defensive Line:

Dave Fennell

Ron Estay

Leroy Blugh

David Boone

Linebackers:

Willie Pless

Danny Kepley

Dan Bass

Defensive Backs:

Larry Highbaugh

Malcolm Frank

Joe Hollimon

Ed Jones

Shannon Garrett

Kicker/Punter:

Dave Cutler

Hank Ilesic

Kick Returner:

Henry Williams

All-Purpose:

Jackie Parker

Coach:

Hugh Campbell
(also selected
as receiver to
the Saskatchewan
Roughriders'
All-Century Team)

CENTENNIAL GRIDIRON CHALLENGE
Sept. 18, 2005 • Oct. 15, 2005

This page: Alberta's Lieutenant Governor and former Edmonton Eskimo running back Norman Kwong (centre) presents the trophy for the Centennial Gridiron Challenge, which ended in a tie between the Edmonton Eskimos and the Saskatchewan Roughriders. Players Jeremy O'Day (l.) and A.J. Gass (r.) accepted the trophy for their teams.

Opposite: Team Alberta defeated Team Saskatchewan in the Centennial Cup Hockey Challenge.

Buffalo Twins

Over 250 visual artists, musicians, athletes, and others applied their talents to creating a massive mural celebrating Alberta and Saskatchewan's Centennials. The mural, entitled *Buffalo Twins*, was first assembled on the ice surface at West Edmonton Mall's Ice Palace. It then toured the two provinces and made an appearance at Alberta Scene in Ottawa.

Hitting the trail for the Centennial

The Trans Canada Trail Centennial Relay 2005 celebrated recreational trails and the Alberta and Saskatchewan Centennials. The relay covered 1,100 km of trails from Edmonton to Regina and passed through 17 communities in Alberta and 37 in Saskatchewan. Flag bearers of all ages carried the Centennial Relay flag from community to community on a variety of permitted trail transport including foot, bicycle, roller blades, horseback, covered wagon and even Red River cart!

Communities double their fun

Several Alberta communities had twice the reason to celebrate in 2005. Among communities marking their own centennials were Camrose, Athabasca, High River, Taber, Claresholm and Olds.

High River erected a bronze statue celebrating High River's and Alberta's 100th birthdays. Claresholm held poster, essay, poetry and song contests for school children to highlight the area's rich heritage and threw a Centennial Homecoming.

Olds held an international town crier competition and put on a re-enactment of the 1907 Battle of Olds between the CPR and townspeople over the closing of a railway crossing. Camrose's Founders Day event celebrated the arrival of the first train to the community (then known as Sparling) in 1905.

Millarville race track also celebrated its 100th year.

Opposite: Imagery in the massive *Buffalo Twins* mural represents the various artists' personal connections to Alberta and Saskatchewan.

This page: 1. Participants in the Trans Canada Trail Centennial Relay 2005. 2. A float in Claresholm's Centennial Homecoming parade. 3. Town crier contestants and their escorts at the at Olds Centennial Homecoming celebrations. 4. Residents of Camrose celebrating Founders Day in period style.

Centenarians honoured

Imagine being here right from the start! Albertans who were born the same year Alberta became a province received special attention in 2005. Seniors turning 100 or older during Alberta's Centennial year were presented with Centennial Medallions to commemorate the occasion.

"I met five ladies who, like Alberta, celebrated 100th birthdays. One told me about her wedding in 1920 – public consumption of alcohol wasn't acceptable then. So the men would hide their private stash of home brew in the stooks in a farmer's field adjacent to the hall. Laughing, she told me that the real winner in this was the threshing crew a few days later because most men, after a few shots, couldn't remember where they hid the bottles."

VIC SADLOWSKI, CENTENNIAL AMBASSADOR, BONNYVILLE

A century of farming and ranching

A special edition of the Century Farm & Ranch Award recognized Alberta farm families who celebrated their 100th anniversary along with Alberta in 2005. Among those honoured was the family of Sarah and William Wallace, who settled to farm in Springbank in 1905 and shortly later moved to Brushy Ridge.

Regiment turns 100

The South Alberta Light Horse Regiment, one of Western Canada's oldest militia regiments, celebrated its 100th anniversary alongside Alberta. A special exhibition mounted at the Provincial Museum of Alberta — *Hoof Prints to Tank Tracks* — highlighted the regiment's contributions to the political, economic and social life of Alberta during the province's first century.

"We must remember to tell our ancestors' stories to our children and grandchildren. Every family has a story. John Steinbeck said it best: 'How will our children know who they are if they don't know where they came from?'"

WALLACE FAMILY MEMBER

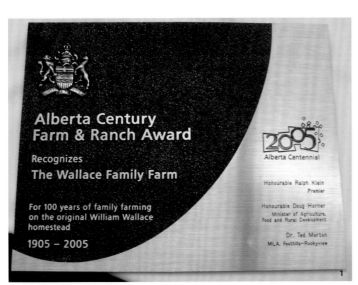

Opposite: 1. Fong Ping Mah turned 110 on September 10. 2. Centenarian Evelyn Smith received her Alberta Centennial Medallion from her son, Centennial Ambassador Ted Smith. Evelyn (since deceased) is shown here with her son and daughter after the ceremony.

This page: 1 & 3. Photos tell the story of the Wallace family, who celebrated the 100th anniversary of the farm started by their ancestors in 1905. 2. The South Alberta Light Horse Regiment – front: Sgt. Joe Walmsley; back (l. to r.): Sid Black, I. Smith, Sam Hoarle, Art Rice.

Souvenirs and Honours

Albertans collected a host of keepsakes that will bring back fond memories of their province's 100th birthday for years to come. Many received special Centennial awards and medals honouring their contributions to the province. Alberta's oldest and youngest residents received medallions commemorating the big year, while newlyweds and new parents received commemorative certificates. All Albertans had opportunities to take home Centennial memorabilia ranging from specially minted coins and stamps to Alberta 2005 wrapping paper, T-shirts and even hot sauce.

Celebrating extraordinary Albertans

Albertans took great pride in celebrating each other's contributions to the province.

Alberta Centennial Medals were awarded to almost 8,000 of the province's most extraordinary men, women and youth whose achievements have benefited their fellow citizens, their community and their province. This one-time award is included in the Canadian Order of Precedence of orders, decorations and medals and can be worn in conjunction with other official honours.

The Alberta Centennial Salute for Sport and Recreation was presented to 100 sport builders from the past century for their outstanding contributions to the development of sport and recreation in the province. Recipients of the one-time award were chosen from communities across the province for having made a tremendous impact on the lives of others through their involvement as athletes, coaches, builders and leaders.

Recipients of Alberta's 100 Great Kids Awards went down in history with the unveiling of the Great Kids Wall of Honour in the Legislature pedway. The awards recognize amazing Alberta children and youth for such accomplishments as overcoming health obstacles, helping others and being positive role models.

"I decided to give back to Alberta because Alberta has been so good to me."
IRENE PFEIFFER, OKOTOKS AREA, ALBERTA CENTENNIAL MEDAL RECIPIENT

"My happiest moments came from helping people."
BEV NEW, PRESIDENT, REGION 5, MÉTIS NATION OF ALBERTA, ALBERTA CENTENNIAL MEDAL RECIPIENT

"It makes you feel like you made a difference."
JORDAN LEE, 17, CAMROSE COUNTY LEADERS OF TOMORROW, MEMBER OF 3068 SOUTH ALBERTA LIGHT HORSE, GRADE 12 STUDENT (2005) AT BASHAW SCHOOL, ALBERTA CENTENNIAL MEDAL RECIPIENT

Opposite: 1. Calgary-Hays MLA Art Johnston presents an Alberta Centennial Medal to Calgary firefighter Terry N. Larson, a Canadian Forces Reserve Officer since 1995. 2. Lieutenant Governor Norman Kwong presents an Alberta Centennial Medal to Bunny Ferguson.

This page: 1 & 3: The Alberta Centennial Salute for Sport and Recreation honoured 100 sport builders from the past century. Lisa Miller and Ken Newans were MCs at the award luncheon. 2. Family and friends of Alberta's 100 Great Kids Award winners witness the unveiling of the Great Kids Centennial Wall of Honour. 4. Evan MacLachlan proudly celebrates the Alberta Centennial Medal awarded to his father, Graham MacLachlan, of Calgary. Constable Jean A. Whyte, a Community Liaison Officer with the Calgary Police Service, also received a Centennial Medal.

Keepsakes

Alberta honoured the contributions of its oldest citizens and the promise of its youngest with commemorative Centennial Medallions. All school children from kindergarten through Grade 12 – approximately 600,000 – received special-edition brass medallions. Approximately 500 Albertans aged 100 years or older in 2005 were given a special 14-karat gold version. Visiting dignitaries received silver medallions. A brass version of the medallion was available for purchase as a souvenir. The Government of Alberta also presented gold medallions with special certificates to each Royal Canadian Legion.

All Albertans born or married in 2005 received commemorative certificates. Certificates went out to approximately 40,000 newborns and 17,000 married couples over the year.

The Royal Canadian Mint coined its own tribute to Alberta's Centennial – a circulation quarter. Albertans got to vote for one of four designs created by Alberta artists. More than 26,000 people put in their two bits.

Canada Post issued a new 50-cent stamp celebrating the province's 100th birthday. The Alberta stamp features pictures of a natural gas plant near Fort Saskatchewan, the Calgary skyline and Mount Lawrence Grassi looming over a CPR freight train.

Cards for collecting

The Provincial Archives of Alberta called up some striking historical images for a new phone card collection honouring Alberta's Centennial. The 16 images included steamers, rodeos, landmarks and portraits of famous Albertans. The phone cards were a joint venture with the Alberta Hotel and Lodging Association and OPCOM Hospitality Solutions Inc.

Travel Alberta launched a Centennial rewards program, issuing one million free holiday cards giving access to travel specials and holiday package offers.

Kathleen Alice Mary Smith-Jones
June 14, 2005
Commemorative Certificate of Birth

PREMIER OF ALBERTA

CANADA
25 cents
ALBERTA
1905 - 2005

ALBERTA CENTENARY   CENTENAIRE DE L'ALBERTA
1905   2005   1905

"The medallion recognizes that there are a century of people to thank for Alberta's success today."

PREMIER RALPH KLEIN

TravelAlberta.com

100 years

CENTENNIAL
ALBERTA
1905-2005

2005 Alberta Centennial

2005 Alberta Centennial

2005 Alberta Centennial

Opposite: 1. Commemorative Certificate of Birth. 2. Alberta Centennial circulation quarter. 3. Silver Centennial Medallion. 4. Canada Post's 50-cent stamp celebrating Alberta's Centennial.

This page: 1. Education Minister Gene Zwozdesky holds up the gold medallion presented to centenarian Eric Schultz. 2. Premier Ralph Klein presents a gold Centennial Medallion to Ruth Cruickshank. 3. Travel Alberta's Centennial rewards program holiday card. 4. Phone cards in the collection launched by the Provincial Archives of Alberta and partners. 5. The front of the Centennial Medallion illustrates Alberta's natural beauty, its people, its heritage and its many gifts; the back features Alberta's coat of arms.

Party favours

What's a birthday party without party favours? The Alberta 2005 Centennial Initiative provided promotional items for Centennial-themed events. Over seven million promotional items were distributed. Numerous Alberta-based companies created clothing, caps, pins, mugs, banners, flags — even chocolate bars, soaps, hot sauce and wrapping paper — to mark Alberta's Centennial and give Albertans something to remember it by.

Lasting Legacies

Well in advance of the big year, the Alberta government asked Albertans how they wanted to mark the province's Centennial. Albertans responded loud and clear: they wanted more than a big party and spectacular fireworks. They wanted to leave a lasting legacy for generations to come. Albertans did this in many ways, large and small, individually and collectively. Now, as they look back on rosy memories of their Centennial year, Albertans are also enjoying new public facilities, scholarships and works of art that will serve future generations well into the province's second century.

Investing in the future

The Government of Alberta invested more than $500 million in 536 legacy projects in 400 communities across the province. The Alberta Centennial Legacies Grant Program contributed $114 million toward 103 community projects such as recreation centres, museums and theatres. Over $200 million was committed to 11 provincial projects for legacies that all Albertans can enjoy.

In addition, $10 million was allocated through the Alberta Centennial Per Capita Municipal Grant Program to help all of Alberta's incorporated municipalities – from First Nations and Métis Settlements to summer villages and major cities – to create meaningful local projects that will leave a legacy in their own special way.

By creating these lasting legacies for future generations, Albertans began the province's second century with a renewed sense of pride and optimism.

This page: 1. EPCOR Centre for the Performing Arts. 2. Grande Prairie Museum. 3. Blackfoot Gallery, Glenbow Museum. 4. Community Sports Fields, Crowsnest Pass.

Opposite: 5. Lakeside Leisure Centre, Brooks. 6. Bow RiversEdge Campground and Recreation Park, Cochrane. 7. Rudy Swanson Park, Camrose.

"My most memorable moment was the opportunity to chair the official opening ceremonies of the Fairview Aquatic Centre... A great big thank you to the Province of Alberta for making a dream come true for the Town of Fairview and area."

LARRY CHORNEY, CENTENNIAL AMBASSADOR, FAIRVIEW

Alberta Centennial Legacies Grant Projects

Communities throughout Alberta are enjoying new or renovated public facilities made possible by contributions from the Alberta Centennial Legacies Grant Program. They include:

AIRDRIE
East Lake Recreation and Wellness Centre

ATHABASCA COUNTY
Athabasca Regional Multiplex

BARRHEAD
Barrhead Sports Grounds

BEAVERLODGE
Beaverlodge Public Library

BLACKFALDS
Blackfalds Leisure Centre

BONNYVILLE
Bonnyville and District Centennial Centre

BROOKS
Lakeside Leisure Centre

CALGARY
Online Access to Alberta's Archives

Calgary Gymnastics Centre

Calgary Rotary Challenger Park

Calgary Zoo – Destination Africa

Cardel Place for Community, Sports and Recreation

EPCOR Centre for the Performing Arts

Glenbow Museum – Blackfoot Gallery, Mavericks Gallery and Permanent Galleries

Haultain Park

Heritage Park Pavilion and Gateway

Talisman Centre

CAMROSE
Rudy Swanson Recreation Park

CANMORE
Canmore Recreation Centre

CARDSTON
Cardston Tourist Information Centre

CHESTERMERE
Chestermere Regional Community Centre

CLARESHOLM
Louise Crummy McKinney Centre and The Bridge at Claresholm Golf Course

COALDALE
2005 Natural History Centre

COCHRANE
Bow RiversEdge Campground

Cochrane Arena

COLD LAKE
Cold Lake Energy Centre

CORONATION
Coronation Community Centre

CROWSNEST PASS
Community Sports Fields

DIDSBURY
Didsbury Exhibition Grounds

DRAYTON VALLEY
Drayton Valley and Brazeau Multi-Purpose Field House

EDMONTON
Alberta Online Encyclopedia

Citadel Theatre

Fort Edmonton Park – Hotel Selkirk

Francis Winspear Centre for Music – Davis Pipe Organ

TransAlta Arts Barns

Londonderry Arena

Louise McKinney Riverfront Park

Northgate Lions Senior Citizens Recreation Centre

Strathcona Library Restoration and Expansion

Traditional Burial Grounds and Fort Edmonton Cemetery

Valley Zoo

FAIRVIEW
Fairview Regional Aquatic Centre

FALHER
Falher Regional Recreation Complex

FORT MACLEOD
Fort Macleod Centennial Legacy Project

FORT MCMURRAY
Oil Sands Discovery Centre

Timberlea Athletic Park

FORT SASKATCHEWAN
Dow Centennial Centre

GRANDE PRAIRIE
Centre for Creative Arts

Grande Prairie Museum and Heritage Discovery Centre

Grande Prairie Gymniks Gymnastics Centre

HANNA
Hanna and District Community Swimming Pool

HIGH PRAIRIE
High Prairie Regional Aquatic Centre

HINTON
Hinton Municipal Library and Archives Renovation and Expansion Project

HUSSAR
The Hub

HYTHE
Hythe and District Memorial Arena

INNISFAIL
Centennial Park

LA CRETE
La Crete Heritage Centre

LAC LA BICHE
Lakeland Interpretive Centre and Regional Leisure Complex

Notre Dame des Victoires Mission Convent Restoration Project

LACOMBE
Lacombe Memorial Centre

LEDUC
Black Gold Centre

Canadian Petroleum Interpretive Centre

LETHBRIDGE
Galt Gardens

Lethbridge Outdoor Soccer and Rugby Complex

Nord-Bridge Seniors Centre

Galt Museum and Archives

LLOYDMINSTER
Common Wealth Centre

MAYERTHORPE
Grain Elevator

MEDICINE HAT
Esplanade Arts and Heritage Centre

Medalta Potteries and Hycroft China

180

Opposite: 1. Notre Dame des Victoires Mission Convent, Lac La Biche. 2. Esplanade Arts and Heritage Centre, Medicine Hat. 3. Olds Aquatic Centre. 4. La Crete Heritage Centre. 5. Hotel Selkirk, Fort Edmonton Park.

This page: 6. Tri-Municipal Family Leisure Facility, Stony Plain, Spruce Grove, Parkland County. 7. Métis Crossing, Smoky Lake. 8. Francis Winspear Centre for Music – Davis Pipe Organ, Edmonton. 9. Dow Centennial Centre, Fort Saskatchewan. 10. TransAlta Arts Barns, Edmonton.

MORINVILLE
Morinville Agriplex

OKOTOKS
Foothills Centennial Centre

Okotoks Recreation Centre

OLDS
Olds Aquatic Centre

PEACE RIVER
Centennial Parks, Playgrounds and Trails

PEAVINE
Peavine Arena and Recreation Park

PINCHER CREEK
Lebel Mansion Legacies Project

PONOKA
Ponoka Community Golf Club

Ponoka Stampede Agriculture Building

PROVOST
Bodo Archaeological Sites Interpretive Facilities and Provost and District Museum

RED DEER
Alexander Way and Centennial Plaza Park

ROCKY MOUNTAIN HOUSE
Rocky Mountain House Swimming Pool

ST. ALBERT
St. Albert Leisure Centre

Ted Hole Park

ST. PAUL
Golf Club

SHERWOOD PARK
Centre in the Park – Prairie Walkway

Millennium Place

SIKSIKA FIRST NATION
Blackfoot Crossing Historical Park Interpretive Centre

SMOKY LAKE
Métis Crossing

STETTLER
Stettler Leisure Centre

STIRLING
Galt Historic Railway Park

STONY PLAIN, SPRUCE GROVE, PARKLAND COUNTY
Tri-Municipal Family Leisure Facility

STRATHMORE
Centennial Aquatic and Civic Centre

SYLVAN LAKE
Sylvan Lake Multi-Purpose Facility

TABER
Taber Public Library

VEGREVILLE
Vegreville Centennial Library

VERMILION
Vermilion Community Cultural and Community Facility

VULCAN
Vulcan Community Golf Course and Walking Path Project

WAINWRIGHT
Peace Memorial Multiplex

WHITECOURT
Spruceview Heights Lodge

Alberta's Provincial Legacy Projects

To provide a birthday gift that all Albertans can enjoy, the Government of Alberta invested in a number of capital projects.

These projects preserve the heritage of Alberta, provide educational opportunities and produce economic benefits by attracting visitors to our communities.

Edmonton – Royal Alberta Museum

Alberta's Royal Alberta Museum will be expanded and will tell the Alberta story through its new permanent galleries including a children's gallery. It will host international touring exhibitions and invite visitors "backstage" into an "Information Zone" to see the museum's collections and workspaces.

Edmonton – Provincial Archives of Alberta

The Provincial Archives of Alberta officially opened its new state-of-the-art facility in a renovated building on Edmonton's south side in October 2003. The facility includes 85 kilometres of shelving in 20 storage vaults located on two floors with specialized environmental controls. The new archives also features a reference and reading room, library, small conference centre, exhibit area, conservation laboratory, processing areas and staff offices.

Edmonton and Calgary – Jubilee Auditoria

In 1955, Alberta's 50th anniversary, the Province of Alberta presented the people of Alberta with two identical Jubilee Auditoria – in Edmonton and Calgary. To mark Alberta's Centennial, the province renovated and refurbished the auditoria to meet the technical requirements of a new century. The Friends societies contributed to the renovation project. The auditoria reopened with gala Centennial performances on September 1.

Opposite: 1. Renovated main hall in the identical Northern and Southern Jubilee Auditoria. 2. Royal Alberta Museum, Edmonton. 3. Provincial Archives of Alberta.

This page: 4. Lougheed House, Calgary. 5. Dinosaur Provincial Park Visitor Centre and Tyrrell Field Station. 6. ATCO Tyrrell Learning Centre, Royal Tyrrell Museum, Drumheller.

Drumheller – Royal Tyrrell Museum ATCO Tyrrell Learning Centre

The ATCO Tyrrell Learning Centre adds more than 16,000 square feet to the museum and allows the museum to go beyond its walls and reach teachers and students around the world. The new wing, which opened in 2003, features three learning zones, a hands-on workshop, a distance learning studio, and an outdoor interpretive area.

Calgary – Lougheed Residence

Lougheed House, also known as Beaulieu, was built in 1891 for Senator James Lougheed and his wife Isabella Hardisty, grandparents of Alberta's eleventh premier, Peter Lougheed. The interior and exterior of this designated National Historic Site were restored as a Centennial project and reopened in 2005. The elegant sandstone mansion symbolized the prosperity that followed the arrival of the Canadian Pacific Railway in 1883.

Dinosaur Provincial Park – Visitor Centre and Tyrrell Field Station

Dinosaurs roamed this area in a lush subtropical landscape 75 million years ago. Today, Dinosaur Provincial Park preserves Canada's largest badlands habitat. The expanded field station in this UNESCO World Heritage Site includes a visitor centre that features exhibits on the outstanding badlands landscapes and habitats within the park. The centre also provides interpretive and environmental education programs.

Lesser Slave Lake Provincial Park – Boreal Centre for Bird Conservation

Lesser Slave Lake Provincial Park is in the migratory path of many bird species from southern Mexico, Central and South America, and the West Indies. The park has been home to Canada's northernmost migration monitoring station – the Lesser Slave Lake Bird Observatory. The new Boreal Centre for Bird Conservation provides laboratory and office space for

scientists, volunteers, and scholars from around the world. It also offers public programs including interpretive exhibits, bird banding demonstrations, ecotourism, and citizen science programs, courses and special events.

Cypress Hills Interprovincial Park – Visitor Centre

Established in 1989, Cypress Hills is Canada's first and only interprovincial park. As the highest point of land in Canada between the Rocky Mountains and Labrador, the hills stand out in the surrounding prairie landscape. The park's cultural heritage includes archeological sites dating back 8,000 years. The park is also home to the Fort Walsh National Historic Site on the Saskatchewan side. The new visitor centre features interactive interpretive exhibits with engaging education and visitor information programs.

Writing-on-Stone Provincial Park – Visitor Centre

Writing-on-Stone Provincial Park is a national historic site and archaeological preserve that protects the largest concentration of native rock paintings and carvings on the North American plains. Hundreds of Aboriginal petroglyphs (rock carvings) and pictographs (rock paintings) are found on the sandstone cliffs of the Milk River Canyon. The new visitor centre features interactive interpretive exhibits and programs on First Nations culture, the North West Mounted Police post, rock art and the awe-inspiring landscape. The programs are presented in conjunction with the Kainai Nation (Blood Tribe of the Blackfoot Nation).

4

5

Opposite: 1. Cypress Hills Interprovincial Park. 2. Boreal Centre for Bird Conservation, Lesser Slave Lake Provincial Park. 3. Landscape feature in Writing-on-Stone Provincial Park.

This page: 4. School group at the Bow Habitat Station. 5. Wind energy is one of the technologies showcased by projects at Alberta Technology Demonstration Sites.

Bow Habitat Station at the Sam Livingston Fish Hatchery

The Bow Habitat Station, located on the bank of the Bow River in the heart of Calgary, is Alberta's first "eco-park". The station includes the Sam Livingston Fish Hatchery, which raises up to three million trout annually for stocking into publicly accessible water bodies. The new interpretive centre offers programs on freshwater aquatic systems, environmental chemistry, water management, fish biology, and more. The 43-acre Pearce Estate Park Interpretive Wetland is an outdoor classroom where school groups can expand their environmental learning.

Alberta Technology Demonstration Sites

Albertans have always been known for their ingenuity. A series of projects showcasing new and innovative technologies in Alberta are being established across the province. The projects focus on the history of the technologies and their significance to Alberta's economy and environment. Examples include wind and solar energy, irrigation technology, and eco-efficient housing.

Centennial Legacies Partnership Projects

The Alberta government undertook a number of legacy projects in partnership with community organizations. They included:

Lieutenant Governor of Alberta Arts Awards Program – Funding to enhance endowments that will recognize individuals for outstanding achievement in the arts in Alberta for many years to come – a partnership between the Government of Alberta, The Lieutenant Governor of Alberta Arts Awards Foundation, the Edmonton Community Foundation and The Calgary Foundation.

Official History of Alberta – Funding to research, write and publish a two-volume history of the province, *Alberta Formed—Alberta Transformed,* a partnership between the government and the Alberta 2005 Centennial History Society.

Wild Alberta Gallery – Construction of a new and innovative gallery at the Royal Alberta Museum. The former Habitat Gallery was replaced by the Wild Alberta display – in partnership with the Federation of Alberta Naturalists. Wild Alberta leads visitors on a journey of discovery examining how human culture is shaping the modern wilderness.

Aboriginal Heritage Grant Program – Funding for Aboriginal groups and local museums to collect, display and interpret cultural objects – a partnership between Museums Alberta and the provincial government.

Main Street Revitalization Projects – Funding for communities to restore local historical resources that revitalize downtown areas into vibrant social and commercial centres – a partnership with the Alberta Historical Resources Foundation, municipalities and community groups.

Alberta Scene – Funding to showcase Alberta talent for 13 days in Ottawa – in partnership with the National Arts Centre, EPCOR, the Government of Canada and numerous other partners.

This page: Lois Hole Centennial Provincial Park protects an internationally renowned region for nesting and migrating waterfowl and shorebirds.

Opposite: 1. The Calgary Exhibition and Stampede received legacy funding for facility upgrades.
2. The new Art Gallery of Alberta will create a dramatic piece of architecture in Edmonton's downtown core.

More exciting legacy projects

To top off the province's Centennial year, the Government of Alberta announced three major legacy projects funded from the 2005 budget surplus:

Calgary Zoo – A bigger elephant house, a new penguin tunnel and a completely renovated conservatory are among the many projects the Calgary Zoo is undertaking with the help of a $35-million grant from the Government of Alberta.

Edmonton Northlands and the Calgary Exhibition & Stampede – Two of Alberta's largest and best known agricultural societies will each receive $35-million for facility upgrades.

Art Gallery of Alberta – The Alberta government invested $15 million in the Edmonton Art Gallery renewal project to create the new Art Gallery of Alberta. The investment recognizes the gallery's growing role in highlighting art, culture and creativity in the province and will create a provincial showcase for art in the capital city.

In recognition of the National Year of the Veteran, the Province made a Centennial investment in the creation of a film that follows a Calgary soldier's experiences at home and on the front lines of World War I. The film culminates in the Battle of Passchendaele, considered by many to be a defining moment in Canada's military identity.

Also in 2005, a new provincial park was dedicated to the memory of Alberta's beloved former Lieutenant Governor Lois Hole. The Lois Hole Centennial Provincial Park protects an internationally-renowned region for nesting and migrating waterfowl and shorebirds.

Investing in people

The Alberta government also invested in Alberta's people by creating legacies in the form of an education savings plan and new scholarships to commemorate Alberta's milestone year.

The Alberta Centennial Education Savings Plan makes available $500 towards a Registered Education Savings Plan (RESP) for every child born to or adopted by Alberta residents in 2005 and after. Subsequent grants of $100 will be available to children attending school in Alberta at ages 8, 11 and 14, starting in 2013. The Alberta Centennial Education Savings Plan is the first provincial program of its kind in Canada.

The government also established scholarships and awards that will keep giving to talented Albertans each year in perpetuity. The Alberta Award for the Study of Canadian Human Rights and Multiculturalism provides one award of $10,000 each year to a graduate student attending school in Alberta whose area of study will contribute to the advancement of human rights, cultural diversity and multiculturalism.

The Alberta Centennial Scholarships Program, launched by the Government of Alberta as a Centennial gift to Canadians, will provide 325 scholarships annually to post-secondary students across the country.

Art School: 2024
(Started saving yet?)

Veterinary School: 2028
(Started saving yet?)

GET A $500 HEAD START.

The Government of Alberta will contribute $500 to help you start saving for your newborn's post-secondary education.

$500 HEAD START.
lberta will contribute $500 to help you
newborn's post-secondary education.

Alberta 2005
Supporting Albertans' drive to learn

Living legacies

As if Alberta wasn't beautiful enough! Communities all over the province created heritage gardens that will delight residents and visitors far into the future. Answering an invitation by Communities in Bloom, residents contributed plants that had been handed down in their families for generations.

Alberta Environment left a living legacy that not only beautifies the landscape but cleans the air, offers shade and provides habitat for wildlife. Starting in 1999, the department provided Centennial trees and shrubs to non-profit organizations for planting on public lands including seniors' lodges, community leagues, and school grounds. In 2005, Alberta Environment planted 3,540 trees and shrubs across Alberta in partnership with Rotary International 5360.

Quilting up a storm

Albertans of all ages stitched up legacy quilts to leave warm memories for future generations. Families in Millet designed their own squares to be sewn into a Centennial community quilt. Students and teachers at Carbon High School in Carbon created a heritage quilt that will be displayed in the school for generations to come. Members of the Alberta Women's Institute made a Centennial quilt depicting 100 years of Alberta history to grace the Alberta Legislature pedway during 2005.

Opposite: Every child born to or adopted by Alberta residents in 2005 and after became eligible for benefits under the Alberta Centennial Education Savings Plan.

This page: 1. These students in Hanna left a living legacy by planting Centennial trees provided by Alberta Environment. 2. Members of the 2005 Alberta Women's Institute Council display the Centennial quilt that AWI presented to the Government of Alberta. Front row (l to r): Phyllis Kosik, Mildred Luz; back row (l to r): Blanche Cunningham, Darlene Wicks, Fern Killeen, Irene Moir, Alice Lowis.

Something to remember us by

A mammoth steel time capsule went on a province-wide tour offering more than 200 communities a chance to give future Albertans something to remember us by. Containing lights, strobes, LED screens and fog machines, the Alberta Centennial Time Capsule visited the 10 AlbertaSpirit communities throughout the summer, ending up September 1 at the official Centennial celebrations at the Legislature in Edmonton.

At each stop on the tour, representatives from surrounding communities deposited "micro time capsules" containing historical mementos, photographs, newspaper clippings, and other items reflecting local culture and history. The travelling time capsule was escorted by a man in period costume driving a 1914 McLaughlin touring car to represent the past and a young woman representing the future. The time capsule also toured Alberta schools in the fall.

The Centennial Time Capsule will rest for the next 100 years at the Royal Alberta Museum. It will be opened in 2105, at Alberta's big bicentennial party.

1 & 4: Albertans came out to greet the Centennial Time Capsule at each stop on its province-wide tour. 2. A young Albertan leaves a message to the future in the Alberta Centennial Birthday Book at a Time Capsule Tour stop. 3. The Alberta Centennial Time Capsule visited the 10 cities that hosted the AlbertaSpirit celebrations, offering more than 200 communities a chance to help mark Alberta's 100th birthday. 5. A man driving a 1914 McLaughlin touring car escorted the Time Capsule around the province.

Attention future Albertans!

What will Albertans of 2105 find when they open the Centennial Time Capsule? Here's what some communities locked away for future generations to ponder:

- City of Edmonton – poem by Edmonton's poet laureate, Alice Major; two nanochips; description of the city's High Level waterfall

- Hines Creek – a souvenir railway spike

- Fairview – a telephone book as a record of everyone in the community

- Village of Munson – a current water bill and tax notice

- St. Albert – a personal account of the 1989 blizzard, remote car starter

- Drayton Valley – a recording from Big West Country radio

- Claresholm – a photo of the class of 2005 from Willow Creek Composite

- Fort Macleod – a letter from Mayor Shawn Patience "from our time to yours: remember us and think of us often, learn from our mistakes and our triumphs."

TOUR STOPS

Ft. McMurray

Grande Prairie

Cold Lake

Edmonton

Wainwright

Red Deer

Banff

Calgary

Medicine Hat

Lethbridge

"Happy Birthday Alberta. I am a 4th generation Albertan, and very proud of this. When this time capsule is opened I will be 109 years old. I will be best known for my work in the veterinarian field, and my amazing way with animals. I will have changed the lives of many children by teaching them the love of horses and how to ride. You'll find me still living on my ranch with all of my horses."

ENTRY MADE IN THE ALBERTA CENTENNIAL BIRTHDAY BOOK

6

This page and opposite:
1. Some Albertans couldn't resist a close-up look at the interior of the Centennial Time Capsule. 2, 3 & 6: Communities along the Time Capsule tour deposited their messages to the future in micro time capsules. 4. Entertainers in period costume greeted the Time Capsule in Banff, where it stopped off during the Council of the Federation Conference.

5

Messages to the future

Hundreds of Albertans signed the Alberta Centennial Birthday Book at Time Capsule stops, leaving joyful, and often thoughtful, messages to future residents of their province. Here are just a few:

HAPPY 100th BIRTHDAY ALBERTA! I came from Philippines and ALBERTA is my new Home! Way to go… and God bless Alberta!

Hey there, Alberta! I've had a great time touring the province this summer. You're beautiful. Happy Birthday!

Happy birthday, dear Alberta, a place that welcomed me and gave me a home. May you always shine brightly.

Happy Birthday Alberta. I'll be a father this year for the first time and very excited about it. It's been a great year and Alberta has been a wonderful place to live. May it continue to be for the next 100 years!

I am an immigrant from Nicaragua who found peace and new Horizons here in Canada. My Husband Julio and my two kids 6 & 5, Julyssa and Ricardo salute you.

Happy Birthday Alberta!!!!! Hope our Province looks as beautiful for you in 2105 as it did in 2005!

Happy Birthday Alberta! I'm a Palestinian Canadian who has lived here all her life and this place is awesome! I love Alberta and I hope the next century treats her well.

You go, Alberta!!!

Over to you, Canberra!

Albertans are leaving a very special legacy to our friends Down Under. The Australian capital of Canberra is using Alberta as a model for planning its 100th birthday celebrations in 2013. In November 2005, Canberra welcomed a representative from Alberta's Centennial. Happy Birthday, Canberra!

CANBERRA 100

500,000,000	Dollars invested by the Government of Alberta in 536 projects in 400 communities to leave a lasting legacy for generations to come
20,000,000	Number of commemorative circulation quarters released by the Royal Canadian Mint in celebration of Alberta's Centennial
7,000,000	Number of Alberta Centennial promotional items distributed
7,000,000	Number of hits to the Alberta Centennial website by the end of 2005
600,000	Number of school children who received Centennial Medallions acknowledging the promise of Alberta's youngest citizens
250,000	Number of Albertans who participated in AlbertaSpirit Centennial celebrations on September 1, 2005, at 12 locations in 10 communities across the province. Countless others caught the festivities live on television and the Internet.
60,000	Number of Albertans who attended official public events in honour of the Royal Visit of Her Majesty Queen Elizabeth II and His Royal Highness The Duke of Edinburgh, May 23-25
56,000	Number of people who attended performances during Alberta Scene, which showcased 600 Alberta artists in 315 performances in 95 events over 13 days in Ottawa
36,000	Number of Centennial invitations sent by Premier Ralph Klein to people in 110 countries around the world inviting Albertans' friends, families and colleagues to visit Alberta during the Centennial year
20,000	Number of participants from around the world attracted to the World Masters Games in Edmonton in July 2005

13,000   Number of kilometres travelled by the Alberta Centennial Time Capsule in 2005 as it collected the memories and mementos of Albertans from 200 communities across the province. The Time Capsule is almost 6.5 metres (21 feet) long and 1.8 metres (6 feet) in diameter, and weighs more than 1,497 kilograms (3,300 pounds) empty, 2,722 kilograms (6,000 pounds) when full.

8,000   Number of Albertans who were awarded Alberta Centennial Medals recognizing their achievements that have benefited their fellow citizens, community and province

2,000   Number of concert goers who attended 10 free concerts by 30 Alberta musical acts during the Alberta Tracks tour of 10 communities across the province

1,964   Number of community-inspired Centennial events in 300 communities across the province posted to the online Alberta Centennial calendar during 2005

500   Number of centenarians who received Centennial Medallions honouring their contributions to the province

105   Number of Centennial Ambassadors, appointed from communities across the province, who were instrumental in generating interest, momentum and participation in Alberta's Centennial celebrations

40   Number of community events across the province visited by Celebrate Alberta Teams. The talented high school students brought Alberta history alive for audiences through skits, quizzes and games.

Credits

Alberta's Centennial – A Celebration! was published by the Alberta 2005 Centennial Initiative.
Editorial Team: Beryl Cullum, Terry Keyko, Marylu Walters
Design and Production: Vision Design Communications Inc.
Writer/editor: Marylu Walters
DVD Producer: Aquila Productions Inc.
Printing: McCallum Printing Group Inc.

Photos, unless otherwise noted on this page, were provided by:
Government of Alberta
Alberta 2005 Centennial Initiative
Centennial Legacy grant recipients
City of Calgary
City of Edmonton
Edmonton Eskimo Football Club
EPCOR Centre for the Performing Arts
National Arts Centre
Wainwright Star News

The publishers wish to thank the many people and organizations that contributed photographs for this book and throughout Alberta's Centennial year. Special thanks go to the Alberta Centennial Ambassadors who, in addition to their many formal activities and responsibilities, took numerous photographs that appear in this book and many more that will help preserve the memory of Alberta's 100th birthday.

Pages 2 & 3
This Country Canada

Pages 12 & 13
Provincial Archives of Alberta P389

Page 14
Provincial Archives of Alberta B6656

Page 15
1. Provincial Archives of Alberta P6768
2. Provincial Archives of Alberta B37
3. Provincial Archives of Alberta B4884
4. Provincial Archives of Alberta B6000

Pages 16-19
Photographs courtesy of Provincial Archives of Alberta, City of Edmonton Archives, City of Calgary Archives, Glenbow Museum, David Roles and Vision Design Communications

Page 27
1. Provincial Archives of Alberta P6817
2. Provincial Archives of Alberta Pa2001

Page 35
2. Daniel Loewen

Page 38
Calgary Exhibition and Stampede

Page 39
Edmonton Northlands

Page 46
2. John Gibson/CCC

Pages 52 & 53
Calgary Exhibition and Stampede and Tri-Star Digital Ltd.

Page 55
1 & 3: Carrie Caruk
2. Tegan McMartin

Page 57
1 & 3: Sharon Goulet
2. Tim Chamberlin

Pages 148 & 149
Gerry Thomas

Page 152
1. Fred Cattroll
3. Michel Dozois

Page 153
4. Fred Cattroll
7. DualMinds

Page 157
1 & 2: Campus Saint-Jean

Page 163
2. Claresholm Local Press
3. Lorraine Piller
4. Ted Gillespie

Page 189
1. Antionette Wecker
2. Michael Cunningham